NOT ALL KIDS DO DRUGS

Lessons in Drug Prevention:
Handbook One
Proactive Parenting Techniques
Second Edition

By
Miles To Go
Kelly Townsend, M.S. & Jonathan Scott

Not All Kids Do Drugs
Lessons in Drug Prevention: Handbook One
Proactive Parenting Techniques
Second Edition

Ordering can be done at www.milestogodrugeducation.com
Kelly Townsend, M.S. & Jonathan Scott

This book was developed from the Parent Meeting Lecture created by Miles To Go for their Drug Abuse Prevention Lecture Series. Miles To Go is based in Southern California.

The information contained in this book is meant to provide the reader with information for drug abuse prevention purposes only. It is not a substitute for medical advice, diagnosis or treatment. A medical professional should be contacted immediately in cases of substance abuse and possible overdose.

While the authors have made every effort to provide accurate information and internet addresses at the time of publication, neither the publisher nor the authors assume any responsibility for errors or changes that occur after publication.

ISBN: 978-1479276462

Our Philosophy for This Book

Years ago, when we first considered writing this handbook, we decided that most people have little or no desire to curl up with a cup of cocoa and a drug abuse prevention book. We'll never be considered a fun read, and we won't make the Top 10 books to bring to the beach list. We have compiled a selection of the most valuable information in a handbook format that we feel is user-friendly, accessible, and consumable in small blocks of time. This is the first in a series of handbooks that will provide anyone parenting or working with kids the tools needed to support their efforts to keep those kids safe in a world full of drugs.

This book is dedicated to the parents who find time to do the extra work required to raise children in a proactive way. Reading this book automatically qualifies you as one.

Table of Contents

**Part 3: Some Kids Are Going to Use
  Drugs and Alcohol   73-108**

Part 4: How Did You Become the Drug Guys?   109-125

Links and References   126-129

Part 1

Answering the Big Questions

1.1 Don't all kids eventually drink or do drugs?

We might as well start with this common parental assumption—all kids will eventually try drugs, especially alcohol. Since this is our starting point, it's where we'll make our first stand: *not all kids do drugs*! We can't tell you how often a parent in one of our presentations announces that, "All kids are going to do drugs." Without fail, at least a couple of parents who stayed silent in the face of this claim approach us after the event ends to say, "I've never done a drug in my life," or, "I've never had a drink or smoked a cigarette. Does that mean I can't teach my kid about this subject?"

In our drug abuse prevention presentations for parents, we encourage schools and parents to support the nonusers. Unfortunately, people that drink and do drugs (the partiers) tend to be more socially gregarious and outspoken than their non-using peers; and all that bluster and bravado tends to drown out the opinions of the nonusers. In addition, despite all we know about the costs associated with teen drug use and adult drug abuse, many people still perceive users as the cool group. The party people are seen as popular and cool, and they reinforce this image with a language filled with terms nonusers might not understand. This special slang acts to bring the users together and exclude others. They also have an easy time finding like-minded others—they just go to a party, look around--and *voila*--instant peer group. The most vocal members of the party group, the ones that lord their drug knowledge over less exposed members of their class or school, are a special breed. We refer to them as drug bullies. Nonusers tend to be scattered among the chess players, the musicians, the athletes, the rock climbers, and the actors. They often don't socialize as a group, and they have difficulty identifying and supporting each other. These nonusers need encouragement to continue their conscious choice, and we need actively to encourage healthy alternatives to drug use.

A major problem, though, is that a few of these drug bullies don't change when they reach adult age. The parent that stands up and says, "All kids are going to use," may well be nothing more than an adult drug bully. Other parents that don't stand up and insist, "No, they aren't," are still being bullied and may still feel uncool about their lack of drug experience. They have told us repeatedly that they don't feel they have enough knowledge to speak up about the subject because they are not part of the supposed In Crowd. They are the parents that aren't invited to, or choose not to attend, the parties where binge drinking is happening. They also don't attend parties where marijuana is smoked and everyone pretends it's cool as long as their kids aren't around to see it.

We've been teaching drug abuse prevention education in schools for a long time, and one of the things we are sure of is that not all kids do drugs. We've had many students get in touch with us years after they saw our program to tell us they still haven't used drugs. Many are now married and starting families and careers of their own, and they did it without falling prey to the silly notion that all kids are supposed to use drugs as a part of growing up.

Of course, it would be foolish for us to think that out of the 10,000 kids we teach each year not one would drink or get high—far from it. We have also heard from some of those who did choose to drink or use drugs. Several of them told us that they stopped before they got into serious trouble; several others went into rehab sooner than they normally would have because of their knowledge that help was available. Many had friends in trouble and were able to help them find their way out of a bad situation. Unfortunately, there are some students we can no longer hear from; but that we hear of. They are the ones that didn't make it out the other side of the decision to use. They are the ones that died.

A Few Common Variations of the Original Question

1.2   All kids will eventually use, so why not let them do it in the safety of our home?

First, it is impossible to monitor a group of kids who are drinking and using drugs in your home unless you are a trained drug specialist or an ER doctor with all the meds and tools you'll need in your bathroom medicine chest. If you think you will stop them from drinking and driving by taking away their car keys, we can tell you from experience that some of the kids are smarter than you are— they bring a second set of keys. If drunks want to drive, they will drive. Before you have your "safe" party, ask yourself these questions: "Can I tell the difference between a drunken, passed out teenager and a teenager who is in a drug-induced or alcoholic coma?" "How do I know if that teenager has alcohol poisoning?" "Do I know the complete health and addiction history of these people and their families?" "Do I know what other drugs and medications they may have used tonight?" If you don't feel 100% confident about everything mentioned above, then you are not capable of taking care of a group of teen drug and alcohol users.

Actually, if you think about it, even if you are confident about all of the above, you are still not capable of taking care of a group of using teens—there are just too many variables to deal with effectively. With so many balls in the air at the same time, even a pro can miss something important.

A quick Internet search immediately highlights the numerous problems parents encounter when they sponsor teen drinking parties—a stabbing death at one supervised party; an alcohol overdose death at another. Even when teens don't die as a direct result of drinking at parent-sponsored parties, many of these stories describe ambulance trips for unconscious teen drinkers and, occasionally, charges that were filed against the parents for violating the numerous laws against providing alcohol to teens or allowing its use to occur.

If you're tempted to let your child attend a party of this sort, ask yourself: Am I confident that these parents would act in a timely and responsible fashion if my child was the one passed out and possibly lapsing into a coma? They would certainly be aware that their participation in and sponsorship of illegal teen drinking would be frowned upon by the very authorities they would be calling. They may well fail to make the call in an effort to avoid the legal consequences that await them if they do. Their hesitancy may well cost your child his or her life.

1.3 I drank and smoked weed when I was younger, and nothing ever happened to me. Why can't I take care of my children and teach them to use responsibly?

If you think your past use magically enables you to teach your child how to use safely, you are kidding yourself. Are you certain that your kid's drugs are the same drugs you were using 20 or more years ago? A lot has changed since then—the types of drugs that are available; their strength and purity; the way they are taken or used—all this and more has changed since the days of your past use.

In the fall of 2009, a woman approached Jonathan at a parent presentation hosted by one of our schools. She described to him her feelings as she was on her way to her first exposure to our program. She said, "My husband and I were children of the sixties and seventies. We thought that, because of our experiences with drugs and alcohol, we were perfectly capable of dealing with any questions that might arise about drugs. Then I sat through your meeting. As soon as I got into the car after the presentation, I was on the cell phone to my husband, shouting, 'You've got to get to one of these meetings—we don't know sh__!' Since then," she continued, "I've encouraged every parent I know to come when they get the chance. There's just so much new stuff out there. I don't think a lot of people realize that."

We read about and study the subject of drugs regularly and extensively. Almost everyone we talk to is scheduled to the gills—they don't have hours and hours each day to educate themselves about drugs and drug issues. We do it because we love it. We do it because we have made it our job. It's also our job to educate parents and make available a capsule version of what we've learned. A parent presentation is a great place to start, but we also regularly recommend our website, milestogodrugeducation.com, as an excellent starting point.

Now, let's go back to the question. We would also like to ask, "How do you know nothing has physically happened to you as a result of your cigarette, drug and/or alcohol use?" Unless you've had brain scans, liver function tests and lung exams over the years, you have no clear picture of what kind of long term changes resulted from your drug use. Updated drug research has taught us that there are many long-term consequences of drug and alcohol use that in the sixties and seventies we didn't know existed. A lot of new evidence indicates that alcohol plays a role in many forms of cancer[i]—we didn't fully appreciate that a few decades ago. We also know more about permanent brain damage caused by cocaine use. In addition, while almost everyone knows that tobacco is harmful and deadly, a lot of people aren't up to speed on the potential damage done by some of the other smoked drugs like marijuana, methamphetamine, and cocaine.[ii]

Do you want to explain to your children why you are dying prematurely because of party choices you made 40 years ago? We ask you that question because it's one we ask ourselves as we send our daughter off to school. The thought of her being alone because of choices we made decades ago makes our hearts ache. We brought her into this world, and she has loved us without reservation—we don't want to miss the journey that lies ahead! Unfortunately, we may have lost any say we had in that a long time ago.

1.4 What about the way they use alcohol in Europe? Don't they drink at an early age and have no problems with alcohol at all?

We are always fascinated by this question. At first, it seems so rational and logical, but further study reveals the misunderstanding and confusion many people harbor about alcohol use in Europe. We want to first point out what most of you already know—Europe is not a country, it is a continent broken up into many countries; each with its different customs, beliefs, and social systems. Those who point to France as a model for safe alcohol use by young people are misinformed. A recent study showed that while teens in France will use alcohol moderately while in the presence of adults, they abuse it the instant adult supervision is removed or absent.[iii] Most people also aren't aware that French males are significantly more likely than other European males to die early,[iv] and that major contributors to this increased mortality are their extensive use of alcohol and tobacco. It's also important to note that France has an alcoholism rate that is equal to or slightly greater than that of the U.S.[v] It's hard to understand how all this constitutes what the questioners refer to as "no problems with alcohol." Maybe it's just that an alcoholic in a beret looks less devastated than one without a snazzy hat.

Those who want to use Italy as their example have a slightly stronger argument. Italy has traditionally had a lower rate of alcoholism than ours,[vi] despite the fact they allow and encourage the use of alcoholic beverages by children. A few things we must note: (1) in Italy, use by young people is limited almost exclusively to wine that has been diluted with water. (2) This watered wine is understood to be a food product, not an intoxicant. (3) It is used to enhance the experience of other food products, not to get drunk. (4) This wine is usually used at the dinner table, in the presence of parents (and often grandparents, too) with the understanding that use is encouraged but drunkenness is abhorred. Italian society also has traditionally dictated that a drunken teen was not cool--they were offensive. Unfortunately, anecdotal evidence seems to indicate that recently this lack of acceptance of teen intoxication has been muted as Italy becomes less isolated because of their membership in the European Union. We feel they will pay a price for this loss of identity if they allow it to lessen their disapproval of teen drunks.

Here's the kicker, though—we don't live in an Italian society. You may actually be able to reconstruct an Italian model of alcohol use at your own dinner table, but when your children venture out into U.S. teen society they will carry no societal protection or prohibition against drunkenness. They will find themselves deep in a climate of alcohol abuse and the associated risks that culture carries. Anatomically, our children are the same as any other kid from anywhere else on the planet, and although regular light drinking, as is found in Italy, shows no direct negative effect on the livers of those teens, heavy abusive drinking (the type typically exhibited by U.S. teens) is quite hard on a juvenile's liver.[vii] In addition, the frontal lobes of the brain don't typically mature until a person is well into their 20's. These brain regions, where we house many of the functions for planning, memory, judgment, impulse control, and reason are the same regions of the brain that are quickly and profoundly affected by alcohol. Finally, we must note the overwhelming evidence that shows the link between early, regular alcohol use and spectacularly increased rates of alcoholism in adulthood.[viii]

So, can you teach kids to use safely? We think that by telling your kids they can use safely in your home you are teaching them that the risks cited above don't apply to your family—that you are somehow different from everyone else. You teach them to ignore science and biology. You teach them to disrespect their developing brains and bodies. You teach them that common sense and proactive thinking aren't as important as having fun and being the life of the party.

Here's what we think you should teach instead: You can show young people how to drink safely when they are adults by being a safe role model for them now; by not drinking and driving; by not drinking to get drunk; and by not using alcohol as an exclusive way to relax at the end of a rough day. Show them how to have fun and unwind without alcohol, and assure them alcohol will still be there for them when they are old enough to use it safely and moderately. Your actions are more powerful than your words.

1.5 As drug educators, what are some issues you deal with that parents may want to know about?

The lack of treatment facilities for teens is shocking, but not as shocking as how expensive treatment is and how little of its cost is covered by insurance.[ix] We are always looking for good referrals so families and schools can help a young person in trouble with drugs. When it comes to addiction, treatment is always preferable to punishment.[x]

Even more frustrating, though, are the parents, faculty, and administrators who have called us about children or other family members in trouble. Of course, each of these people calls us with the best intentions in mind. All have someone they care deeply about. They are seeking advice and formulating plans of action. Our frustrations usually lie in the fact that virtually all of these people are overwhelmed by how much commitment is required on their part if this outreach is to succeed. Getting someone help is harder than it seems: Who is going to choose the treatment facility? Who will fill out the necessary paperwork? Who will arrange for and make the payments? Who will approach the young person in trouble? What happens if said young person resists these efforts? What happens if they do accept the offered treatment but fail in their attempt to get clean?

In the face of this overwhelming list of complications, even the most dedicated crusaders can lose hope—it's just more trouble and effort than they ever imagined; so they put it on the back burner and hope the problem will go away by itself. We worry about the people who aren't getting the help they need, and wonder how many years will pass before they do get help.

Another issue, mostly faced by parents and family members, is the sense of embarrassment and failure they feel about their loved one's drug problems. Our society has come such a long way in its efforts to make people more comfortable with discussing addiction in the family, but there is more than just a lingering reluctance on the part of many parents to deal with this openly. The problem will not get better if we just ignore it. Throwing your hands in the air and declaring that you have no control over your family situation is not the solution either. It's important to remember that people die from drug and alcohol abuse and addiction. While we all hope it won't happen to our children or us, it sometimes does, and it often does so, at first, in the most subtle ways.

1.6   Adults Should be Present in Drug Education Classrooms

Many drug education programs have for years insisted they be allowed to work without teachers or other adults in the room. Most claimed that the students were more likely to "open up" if there were no adult representatives from the community present; that the discussions would be ruined if they could not be done in private. We feel exactly the opposite is true, and worry about what actually occurs in that privacy.

The only thing that happens in our classrooms is drug education. Whatever form the discussion takes, it is certainly not therapy or a twelve-step meeting. The assumption that we need privacy indicates that something secret is going on. Even if the privacy did allow for open disclosure of behavior that would trouble an adult from the community, we don't want the burden of deciding which secrets to keep and which to disclose. We think it a bit disingenuous to invite open discussion and then reveal those secrets to faculty and administration under the guise of caring, and yet that is what would be required of us if we were to find out something that represented a danger to a student or community member.

We also believe that school-based drug education programs will not solve the drug problem all by themselves— they are just one piece of the puzzle. When teachers sit in on our lectures, they experience the same class the students do. Because everyone is on the same page, ongoing discussions about drug issues can continue well after we've moved on. We think these discussions also dovetail well with the conversations that happen in the homes of parents who attend the parent section of our visit. We eagerly await feedback from teachers about how they use our new homework page on our website in their efforts to engage students in life skills discussions.

The other thing teachers add to the experience is another set of adult ears. Kids are extremely selective listeners, but even when they can repeat verbatim what was said, they often interpret the meaning of what was said differently than what was intended. We think it's critical that teachers be able to clear up misunderstandings and gently correct mistakes when they arise. The last thing we need is more misinformation about drugs being passed off as fact because, "That's what the drug guy said." In addition, if parents ever need clarification of what was discussed, the teacher will be perfectly able to do the job.

1.7 Students are Selective Listeners

Another challenge, one we're sure we have in common with just about every teacher on the planet, is the amazing ability of students to listen selectively. We're convinced that the vast majority of the misunderstandings that occur are attributable to simple listening problems or distractions that occur at the most inopportune moments, but sometimes kids just want to twist the tail of a parent or teacher.

An example of the latter occurred when one of our contacts, the school nurse, got a call from a parent who questioned the appropriateness of Kelly teaching drug education despite the fact that she was smoking marijuana as a part of the treatment she was undergoing for cancer. The nurse, a very good friend of ours, asked, "Kelly, is there something you want to tell me?" Further investigation revealed that all this misinformation was the product of one fifth-grade boy's effort to start some drama. Kelly didn't have cancer, nor was she smoking medical marijuana for any reason— this young man just made it all up based on a few things he had heard during the medical marijuana discussion in the class. While trying to repair the damage done by this young man's tales, Kelly and the nurse found that this simple lie had caused quite a bit of upset among the rest of the class—half of them were really worried about Kelly, and the other half were freaked out that they were being taught by someone who was smoking marijuana.

1.8 Parental Fear can Elicit Irrational Behavior

Drug education can bring out some strong emotional reactions in parents. It's perfectly understandable that they would be uneasy, even fearful when their children receive information on such a sensitive topic. Occasionally, though, this fear can be inspired by deliberate attempts to cause a stir, as was the case when a teenage son was out for some laughs at his mom's expense. At an evening meeting a number of years ago, a woman homed in on Jonathan the minute she came through the door. She quite seriously demanded to know why her son would come home from drug education and tell her that it was OK to take cocaine to treat his ADHD. Of course, one minute of rational thought would have helped her understand that any drug educator who made that statement would be quickly and permanently out of work, but this mom wasn't thinking rationally—she was terrified that some stranger was putting her son in danger. If Jonathan had actually said what she thought he had, the danger to her son would have been real, but it wasn't—the whole thing was created by a bored kid who wanted to fire things up a little.

Another child did almost exactly the same thing, and as it turned out, for almost exactly the same reason. On the way home from school, this student told his mom that Jonathan said, "It's OK to do drugs as long as you don't get addicted." The mom immediately called the school and demanded to know what was going on. A couple of phone calls later, it was determined that the student knew that we never said anything of the sort—he was just heating up his mom.

Each of these anecdotes points to a common theme we see repeatedly as drug educators—people are justifiably afraid of drugs and what those drugs can do to their loved ones. Unfortunately, scared people act irrationally, and irrational people are hard to stop once they get on a roll. The damage they do before they calm down may be hard to fix, and things they say may be hard to take back. As parents, we get how scary this stuff can be; but we think it's a good idea to move away from the fear of drugs and toward a healthy, knowledgeable respect for them. Maybe then we'll see a little less craziness and a little more reason when we respond to situations that involve drugs, even if those situations are merely the result of a practical joke gone awry.

1.9 Practical Jokes and Drugs are a Bad Mix

Sometimes our more dedicated practical jokers find themselves in hot water over what started as a prank. More than once, we have run across a student who decided it would be cool to bring something to school and pretend that they had drugs. One young man simply collected a bag of grass clippings and told his classmates he had marijuana. Another gathered up chalk dust in a baggie and claimed it was cocaine. More ominous, since a real drug was masqueraded as another more powerful one, was the time a student brought No-Doz (potent caffeine tablets) to school and declared them to be ecstasy.

In the first two cases, the students were unpleasantly surprised to find that they had violated their respective schools' drug policies. Since there was no real drug involved, neither of these students was expelled, but both had the opportunity to ponder the consequences of their actions as they served their suspensions. In the last case, there existed a real potential for disaster. Granted, there is only one documented case of caffeine overdose that resulted in death that we are aware of, but hospital and poison control center records across the country are full of reports documenting adverse reactions to caffeine tablets. Some of these patients were admitted to the ICU due to the severity of their symptoms. The student in the last example unwittingly created a real danger, and was lucky to remain enrolled.

1.10 Schools Need Clearly Outlined Drug Policies

One final point we want to make about issues we face at work concerns schools that lack clearly outlined policies about how they deal with drug and alcohol issues in their communities. We have learned that unless schools adequately delineate their policies and responses to situations that involve drugs and alcohol, they will find themselves reacting to each new calamity without proper consideration. It has been our experience that unplanned and unpracticed responses, or no response when one is required, have the potential to end in disaster.

One such case involved a parent who regularly showed up at carpool with the odor of alcohol on her breath. The staff didn't know what to do, and there was no policy in place to guide them, so nothing was done to address the problem. Inaction remained the status quo until this parent was leaving the parking lot one day after picking up her kids in carpool. Perhaps a little drunker than normal, she turned too quickly and ended up striking a parking meter in front of the school. We're sure the embarrassment the kids felt as their mom was arrested for DUI in front of the whole school was real and quite distressing. We're sure the mom felt awful and embarrassed about it as well, after she sobered up. Perhaps the most shaken up, though, were all the faculty members and administrators who had let this go on for far too long. Their perceived powerlessness put many people in danger. In the right drunk driving accident those kids, their mom, and any number of other innocent people might have died. That it didn't happen was pure luck.

Unfortunately, this same situation plays out in many different school activities. Sometimes, parents who have had a few drinks arrive to pick up the kids at the school dance. Parents regularly drive away from school fundraising events where alcohol is commonly provided. We're positive that no school wants a parent to get a DUI, but we're also very aware that those schools know that checkbooks come out more easily and the checks written are bigger after those parents get a little drunk. Sometimes they get a lot drunk. There is a mixed message here that concerned school communities are eager to address. If you want a complete list of policies we think schools should discuss and enact, please contact us, or refer to our upcoming handbook, "A Fly on the School Wall."

Parents don't just make mistakes regarding their own behavior—they make mistakes in the name of protecting their children. Most parents act very appropriately when their kids mess up. They realize the potential opportunity for their children to experience the consequences of their behavior and learn from their mistakes. Unfortunately, we've seen more than a few parents try to buy, yell, bully, and sue their way out of their child's rule breaking. Some parents' behavior is simply shocking. One case involved a student dismissed and sent home early from a school trip for an egregious violation of school rules. The parent arranged for the child to be intercepted upon touchdown at a US airport and immediately had him re-board another international flight for a return trip to the same city he just left. The parent also arranged a room at the hotel right next to the one in which the rest of the students on the trip were staying.

The problem is obvious to everyone but the parent and the child. When a kid breaks a rule and the parent does everything in their power to eliminate the consequences, what message does that send about how lives are lived? There is a fine line between protecting your child from harm and going so far that the opportunity to learn from mistakes is lost or intentionally erased.

Part 2

What Parents Need To Know

2.1 Never Underestimate Your Power

Every time we speak to parents at our parent education meetings, the very first point we want to establish is this—never underestimate your power! It's easy for parents to feel less than powerful. It can sometimes seem that the only reason your children even exist is to make you doubt yourself. Many kids are more than eager to recite a list of their parents' inadequacies—you're too strict; you're not cool; you're an embarrassment; you just don't understand! You are the only one in the world who acts like this—other parents let their kids do this or try that. You're the only one with both feet stuck firmly in the mud.

Even if you retain nothing else from this entire booklet, we will consider it a win if you just remember this: you are, by far, the most important influence your children will ever have in their lives. They look to you for all the most important life lessons—values, morals, self-confidence, life skills. You are the last line of defense, the one who will always be standing with arms open, welcoming them in even if the rest of the world has shut them out completely. So many children we meet whose parents have failed to act like parents are bereft. If you won't parent your child, nobody else will.

You can't think it's the job of the school, either. Schools educate in the area of academics. While most of the schools we work with provide adequate time to discuss the intellectual aspects of ethics, life skills, and character, it is the job of the parents to impart values into their children's lives. It is the most important job you will ever do.

There's just one problem—it's so hard to tell if you're doing a good job! One of the most critical mistakes we see parents make is to look to their children for validation of their parenting skills. It is not your children's job to validate you—their job is to make you feel like an idiot! Many years ago, a fellow educator put it perfectly when she said, "Your job is to be the wall; their job is to grind you into gravel." Unfortunately, being a good parent rarely feels rewarding in the short run. A quote in an article in a small Colorado Springs newspaper summed it up by reminding us, "You have to be willing to be uncomfortable. Parenting should be significantly uncomfortable for large periods. And if it's not, you're not doing it right."[xi]

The good news is that if you do your job, if you struggle to parent well for significant periods, you will eventually be rewarded. When? When your kids finally have kids of their own, of course! One of the saddest things in Jonathan's life is that his mom died just four months before our daughter was born. He never got the chance to tell his mom, "Oh! Now I get it! You did all that stuff because you loved me!"

2.2 Communication

When you do talk to your kids, it's a good idea to do your best to communicate as effectively as possible. Don't waste time and energy not getting your message across. Check our recommended reading list at www.milestogodrugeducation.com for some excellent books on communication if you want some guidance from the professionals. In the meantime, practice the most basic communication skill—checking for understanding. When you talk with your children, be sure you understand them and they understand you. After you say something, ask them to repeat back to you what they heard. If they didn't really get your meaning, rephrase your point and try again. When you are all on the same page, your conversation can continue.

Do the same when they say something to you—repeat back to them what it is you heard. You will be surprised, if you've never tried this before, at how often you misunderstand and are misunderstood. While this exercise can be frustrating and time-consuming at first, it is much less frustrating and wasteful than spending a lifetime operating on bad information.

2.3 Start With the Basics

Parents regularly approach us after our parent presentation to talk about specific issues they are dealing with. Often, it feels like what they would like most is an answer—what can they do so this thing will just be fixed? This is a classic good news/bad news situation. The bad news is, there is no answer—drug issues can't be fixed by doing any one thing. The good news is that there are very specific, time-tested things everyone can do that will improve the likelihood of a positive outcome. It's very important to be clear here: you can do all these things, all the time, for a long time, and still have a bad outcome. That does not mean they are not worth doing. Parents who apply these principles consistently are rewarded with seriously lower rates of drug and alcohol use on the part of their children.[xii] We think the worst mistake you can make, though, is to try something once and then give up because it doesn't work the first time. You may need to adjust these ideas to fit your circumstances, but don't quit after one attempt!

Remember, nobody's perfect. We don't think many parents will be able to do all the things we suggest all the time. Choose your favorites and start with those. When you get comfortable with those, try a few new ones. If you have a favorite tip or trick you have found to be effective that you don't see here, send us an email and we'll include it so others may benefit from your wisdom. The important thing is to try. Not to try is to not parent.

2.4 The Big Three

We have a few suggestions that we consider the basics for proactive parents. They are:

- Have an active role in your teenager's life.

- Have a curfew.

- Have a stated policy of non-use.

2.5 Have an Active Role in Your Teenager's Life

Yes, right when it seems your teens want you out of their lives, you have to be in them. Here are a few ideas about what an active role looks like:

a. **Know what's happening at school.** We are not talking about micromanaging children's homework question by question, but we do want you to be aware of what's going on at school. When is the midterm? When is the science fair? When is the play? When is the game? When something big happens, ask how it went. This lets your children know that you appreciate they are busy and you care about how they are doing.

b. **Know your child's friends.** It would be hard to overestimate how important friends are in your child's life. A great friend can change a life, but so can a bad one. If your child has a friend who exhibits behaviors you find troubling, you have to be

27

vigilant about the relationship's effect on your child. A friend who uses drugs is a direct threat to your child, and must be treated as such. Unfortunately, dealing with a bad friend can be a lot like dealing with quicksand—the more you struggle, the deeper and faster you sink. It pays great dividends here to address the *behaviors* that bother you, not the friend as a person. Perceived attacks on a friend will often be read as attacks on your child, so addressing the behaviors can take some of the sting out of the discussion. This much is certain, though—direct evidence of a friend's drug use constitutes direct evidence of that friend's potential to cause your child harm.[xiii] That situation must be addressed directly.

c. Understand, and help your child understand, peer pressure.

"The main consequence of saying no to negative peer pressure is not just withstanding 'the heat of the moment,' as most adults think. Rather, it is coping with a sense of exclusion as others engage in the behavior and leave the adolescent increasingly alone. It is the loss of the shared experience. Further, the sense of exclusion remains whenever the group later recounts what happened. This feeling of loneliness then becomes pervasive but carries an easy solution -- go along with the crowd." **Michael Riera, Uncommon Sense for Parents With Teenagers**

We have made it a formal policy in our classroom never to use the term "peer pressure" until after a student has used it. Peer pressure may be one of the more loaded and misunderstood concepts we deal with. Most adults we meet think there is some monstrous group of adolescents out there actively and aggressively trying to force their child to change and conform. Many young people we meet say they see the term peer pressure, when used by adults, as a two-pronged insult—your friends are out to hurt you; and you are bound, like some sort of brain-damaged sheep, to mimic any behavior you witness. This does not mean we don't see peer pressure as massively powerful, we just think it's much more subtle than most parents think.

As we see it, the most powerful peer pressure is not generated by the peer group, but is more a form of self-talk that constantly assesses situations with an eye toward the idea, "What can I do to make sure I will be accepted?" Most groups will not insist overtly that your child conform, rather they act or speak or dress a certain way, and accept outsiders only if they are willing to do the same. This pressure to conform is much more subtle than the commonly held notion, and yet is no less powerful.

Proactive parents can help their child develop resiliency in the face of peer pressure by reinforcing the idea that the child is a valuable person worthy of thinking and behaving as an individual. Children should be taught that any person who

29

requires them to act a certain way in order to gain acceptance is not worthy of friendship. This effort should start as early as possible and continue throughout the teen years.

d. **Know your child's friend's parents.** No, you don't have to have intimate relationships with the parents of every casual acquaintance in your child's life, but if your son or daughter is going to spend any meaningful amount of time with other parents, you should know them. When your child is with those other parents, on some level these people will act as parents to your child, even if you have never spoken to them. Remember, other parents may not feel the same way you do about some very critical issues. We constantly deal with the issue of parents who feel it is better for kids to drink or use drugs at their house rather than have them do it out on the streets. (We will address this extensively in another section of this handbook.) To us, this is flat out irresponsible, and we can't support it in any way, but you have to be aware these people exist. If your child is in their presence, that child is automatically at risk.

e. **Know what media your child is being exposed to.** What music do your children listen to? What movies have they seen recently? What do they watch on TV? If you don't know the answers to these questions, you may not be doing all you can to keep your children safe. Media have rarely been shown to directly cause drug and alcohol use, but they can create a climate that encourages their use.[xiv] You could literally spend the rest of your life watching youtube videos of kids doing drugs. Continued viewing of these videos by your children probably isn't the best use of their time, and it certainly isn't just an innocent way to while away the hours. It's also important to know which movies and TV programs your children are watching. There is a direct association between the number of R-rated movies your young children or early teens have seen and the likelihood they will smoke, drink alcohol, or do drugs.[xv] The more often your children see smoking in movies, no matter the rating, the more likely they are to smoke.[xvi] By the way, these are not minor differences—the risks increase dramatically as the number of R-rated movies climbs.

f. **Communicate regularly with other adults who have a supervisory role in your child's life.** Think about it—your child's teachers may spend more time with your child during the week than you do. A teacher or counselor may also have information about the groups your child is hanging out with that you can't easily access any other way. If they see variations in behavior or activities that they find troubling, an ongoing relationship with you will make it easier for them to alert you to these important issues.

g. **Eat dinner with your children as often as you can.** The Center for Addiction and Substance Abuse (CASA) at Columbia

University, in a study sponsored by Nickelodeon, showed that the most positive thing you can do is eat dinner with your children. Parents who have dinner with their children five nights each week have children who are 50% less likely to smoke, drink alcohol, or use drugs than do parents who have dinner with their children two nights per week.[xvii] We know—life is complicated, you're busy, but try to make a point of eating dinner with your family as often as you can. You'll be doing great work if you do.

2.6 Have a Curfew

We think it's important here to define what we mean by curfew. A curfew is not necessarily a fixed point in the day, but more a time that adjusts in accordance with what's going on in your child's life that day. The most important things to consider when determining when a curfew should be include what activities will take place and what the approximate transition time is from one place to the next. If the movie ends at 9:20pm, everyone wants to stop for ice cream, and the total drive time between movie, Ben & Jerry's, and home is 30 minutes, it's reasonable to have a 10:45pm curfew.

Having a curfew should not be viewed as you playing the role of time cop—it's about keeping your children in the presence of adult supervision as much as is humanly possible. If they aren't directly in the presence of adult supervision, they should be in transition from one supervised setting to another without a lot of free time. Why? Because young people, especially when they are in groups outside the presence of adult oversight, are much more likely to do something they wouldn't do if there were simply an adult standing there.[xviii]

Curfews should also include the proviso that if any variations from the planned itinerary occur then a phone call must be made to update you on the changes. In addition, if a curfew is going to be missed for any reason, a phone call must let you know why. If changes aren't noted or a curfew is missed without explanation, there should be a pre-arranged series of escalating consequences.

Notice we said the consequences for violating the curfew should be known to your children before any actual violation takes place. Clearly stated and understood consequences for undesirable behavior actually allow your children to consider the costs associated with decisions, and may potentially be used as a valid way for them to avoid participating in actions suggested by the group. (We'll talk more about this later.)

When we speak of consequences, we are not suggesting that when your kids break the rules you must immediately squish them like bugs. Punishment should never be out of context, overly harsh, or so disproportionate as to be unenforceable. Try always to be sure the punishment fits the crime. The worst thing you can do is fire your biggest gun at the first infraction. Really—what do you do after that?

Please note that curfews don't just apply to late at night. We've heard from lots of local police departments about what happens between 3pm and 6pm—the time of day when a lot of parents mistakenly think their children are supervised when they really aren't. Young people who hang around with other unsupervised teens are more likely to have difficulties with drug use, sexual activity, and other undesirable behaviors and emotional difficulties. [xix]

Finally, many parents we meet aren't aware that their towns have curfews for unsupervised teens. The town we live in at the time of this writing has a curfew for all minors that extends from 10pm to 6am. Nobody under 18 can legally be in a public place or on the premises of any establishment without a parent or guardian present. If your town has a curfew, you can discuss it when explaining your curfew rules to your children.

2.7   Have a Stated Policy of Non-Use

We have occasionally sent surveys home with our students. The students are supposed to interview their parents and fill in the answers themselves. We were surprised at some of the answers we got to the question, "Do you have a stated policy of non-use for the children in your family?" Frequently, the handwriting on the answer sheets changed for those particular answers—the adults had apparently taken the answer sheets from the children and started answering in their own handwriting. Often, the answers started with words to the effect, "It should go without saying that drug use is not allowed in this house!"

We want this to be clear: If it goes without saying, it goes unsaid. Children do not realize or understand what their parents want from them unless it is stated clearly and often. We always wonder aloud, "How many times do you have to tell your children to pick up their socks before they actually do it?" Why, then, do some parents think their children will automatically not drink, smoke, or do drugs if that expectation has not been clearly and frequently outlined? We can't overstate the power of parents who regularly voice the desire that their children refrain from drug and alcohol use—parents who do will reduce the chances their children will use by half.[xx]

Some parents think that rules and expectations of non-use will alienate their children. Actually, despite everything your children may say to the contrary, rules and expectations make them feel protected and loved. Parents who try to win the favor of their children by being the "cool parent" or the "pal" are completely missing the point, in our opinion. Years ago, Jonathan was having lunch with a group of juniors when one young man said of another, "His mom is really cool. She lets us drink beer and smoke weed with her." In an absolute deadpan, the other young man said, "I have plenty of friends. What I really wish I had was a real mom." Remember, if you don't parent your children, there is nobody else to fill that spot. You don't have to be mean and unfriendly, but you do have to be the adult. As your children grow into adulthood, the respect you earned by parenting them well will pay the dividend of a lifetime of friendship.

Parents regularly wait too long to have conversations with their kids about drugs. Many seem to think that their kids won't think about drugs if they just don't mention them—they hope the subject never comes up. Actually, the earlier you start the conversations about curfews, expectations and values, the more opportunities you will have to initiate conversation that is in context. Numerous studies show that one of the major reasons teenagers cite for not using drugs is that they don't want to disappoint or embarrass their parents.[xxi] If you let your kids know exactly what you want, they may surprise you—they may do everything they can to meet your expectations!

If you start with these three simple things—have an active role in your child's life, set curfews, and have a stated expectation of non-use—you have laid down a foundation that will allow you to build success after success on top of it. If you don't, or if you have a laissez-faire attitude, then you will probably reap exactly what you sow. The Partnership for A Drug Free America said it beautifully when they penned, "Silence isn't golden. It's permission."

After you've started with the big three, you can move more fully into the rest of the tips we've learned over the years. What follows are techniques and how-to's you might need when certain challenges come up. Again, most people can't do all of them all the time, but keep them in mind and do your best. It's a very powerful list!

2.8 Look for Teachable Moments

A lecture is not a conversation. As an adult, your life experiences can certainly be useful to your adolescent, but unless you can find an effective way to communicate that knowledge, you might as well be talking to a mirror. Effective communication requires that information be both presented and received. A lecture is nothing more than a broadcast. Most students we talk to assure us that a lecturing adult sounds much like the wah wah wah wah of Charlie Brown's teacher. How are we supposed to talk to our kids, then? First, conversations about drugs and alcohol are most effective if they are in context. As drug educators, we are constantly on the lookout for opportunities and settings that call for these discussions.

If your kids watch TV, make an effort to watch with them occasionally. We're amazed at how much underage drinking on TV is depicted as normal. Watch movies with your children, and when you see drug and alcohol use (which you will) try to pay attention to the outcome of the use you see. Are there any consequences that result from the use? Is the use portrayed as cool? Ask your kids if they think that's how it works in the real world. When you see underage drinking, ask them if they know people who act that way, and if they think things in real people's lives usually work out the way they do for characters in a movie or on a TV show.

Listen to the music your children listen to. Are there drug and alcohol references? Why? Do they serve a valid point, or do they serve as a glorification of a drug lifestyle without consequence?

Look for billboards that reference drugs and alcohol in any way, and discuss them with your children. Be mindful to resist the urge to issue proclamations about how bad drugs are; instead, try to remember you are having a discussion. You are trying to understand what your children think rather than trying to make them think just as you do.

With a little planning, you can actually create situations that allow you opportunities to talk to your kids about important issues. For years, we have recommended a website called teachwithmovies.org as a way to foster discussion. For a nominal fee ($11.99/year in early 2010), you can access over 300 insightful film reviews, many with accompanying study guides that will allow you to look way smarter than you may have in past efforts to talk to your kids.

Pay attention to anti-drug ads on TV. When you watch an anti-drug ad, ask your children if they understand what the ad is trying to say—some ads are so abstract even we don't understand their point! Ask your children if they think the ad addresses a real problem, or if it just comes off as preachy. If you don't watch a lot of TV, log on to adgallery.whitehousedrugpolicy.gov to view an extensive list of 30-second drug spots. Some we think are good, others we think are lame, but the important thing here is what do your children think?

One last suggestion for a shared media opportunity—if your kids are old enough, watch a few episodes of the award-winning A&E show "Intervention." We have to warn you, you should watch a few episodes by yourself so you can decide whether you should share them with your children. These are gritty, and there is an overwhelming sense of desperation, sadness and loss that pervades the first three-quarters of each episode. The good news is that almost all the subjects do ultimately go to rehab, but the bad news is the same as it always is with addicts—most of them will fail over time in their attempts to get clean. As you watch the show with your children, please notice how each of the people documented has a complete and utter lack of joy. What they are doing is not fun, and it certainly isn't partying. When you realize that over 60% of young people who use drugs and alcohol cite as their reason for use a desire to "feel good and have fun,"[xxii] this show powerfully highlights how much the reality of what happens to drug users can differ from the perception of what young people think will happen.

Be mindful of time when you try to have drug discussions with your kids. We always tell parents to think of them as discussion drive-bys—get in, talk for a few minutes, then get out! Unless your children are showing signs of absolute engagement, talk with them for a few minutes, and then drop it; after anything more than a few minutes, you run the risk of lecture infection.

2.9 Have a United Front

The classic nuclear family, while desirable, is not the only family structure we deal with. Whatever form your family takes, it's important that the adults present a uniform message when discussing drug issues with their children. If all the adults in a child's life insist on presenting their particular spin on drugs and alcohol to that child, they run the risk of delivering a mixed message. Young people don't thrive in a system built on mixed messages—they need clarity, not confusion. We are not saying you have to agree with each other on all things drug-related, just that you should agree on what is to be said to your children at any given point in their lives.

Years ago, Kelly worked with a family suffering the consequences of mixed messages. The dad, a very successful medical professional, smoked marijuana in college, but all his accomplishments later in life had convinced him that his drug use had caused no measurable damage. The dad was of the opinion that occasional drug use was normal and harmless. The mom, on the other hand, was terrified, because their son had listened to his dad's message and had started his own drug use. Unfortunately, the son's use was different from his dad's—it started at a much younger age, it was much more extensive, and the drugs he was using were more varied and much more potent that those of his dad's era. So, dad says it doesn't really matter, but mom is terrified and wants her son to stop. It's not very hard to understand how the son could migrate toward the dad's viewpoint.

Ultimately, the outcome was positive. After a few months of intense discussion, the dad came to realize how much trouble his son was really in, and eventually even the son realized how much his life was falling apart. Much to the relief of his mom, his very concerned sister, and his new on-board dad, he eventually stopped using. The most powerful factor contributing to his decision to stop using was, to us, the fact that the dad finally stopped validating his son's own drug use. If you and your significant other can only agree on one thing, you should consider this as a top contender—try to find a common ground when discussing drug and alcohol issues with your kids. Obviously, we think this common ground should include the notion that drug use by teenagers is unsafe and unhealthy.

2.10 Create a Family Mission Statement

Yes, you can do this, and no, it is not a lecture! A recent Google search for "family mission statement" yielded 15,700,000 results. This is not a brand new idea—families have long had specific sets of values they believe in and model their lives around, but the notion of creating a document that outlines those values is much more popular now than it was just a few decades ago. On our recommended reading list, we have a number of books and workbooks that discuss how to develop a mission statement for your family, but they barely scratch the surface of what is available to help you. Your mission statement might be a very formal, classically corporate document that you frame and hang on the wall (not really recommended), or it can be a poem you feel accurately reflects the values you want your family to live by, or a picture, or just a few bullet points.

The form it takes is much less important than what the family mission statement accomplishes—it defines the values your family uses to live honorable lives. The positive thing that happens when you identify and state your family values is that you provide your children with foundational values that travel with them wherever they go. If you don't delineate and state your family's values, your children are much more likely to adopt the values of whatever group in which they end up. Remember, not all parents think as you do. If you and your children have agreed to a family value that says, "Alcohol is for people 21 and older," they are much less likely to accept a glass of wine offered by some other kid's parent in their home.

Your family mission statement also gives your children a tool with which they can deflect offers of drugs and alcohol. We don't expect that adolescents will comfortably say, "My family and I have agreed that alcohol is for adults," but they can use that part of the mission statement as the reason for saying, "No thanks, I'm good."

Please don't try to create your mission statement in one burst of effort. You may want to spend 10 minutes a week talking with your kids over dinner about what everyone thinks should represent your family values. One mom recently shared her family's technique for developing a family values statement, and we loved it so much we want to share it with you. Her idea was to have a huge piece of poster-sized paper taped to the refrigerator door. At the top was the title, "How to Be a Smith." (Insert your family name in place of theirs, obviously.) Everyone in the family was welcome to write whatever they thought it meant to be a member of that family. To keep it light and truly focus it on her family, she had written a few funny things on the list to get it started. Since her whole family loves chicken and dumplings, the first entry was, "If you want to be a Smith, you have to love chicken and dumplings." (Once, when Jonathan was presenting our parent meeting with the aid of a translator, we had to stop the meeting because we were laughing so hard when the translator said, in Spanish, "If you want to be a Gonzalez, you have to love menudo.") As the list grew, she started to include more earnest entries about values she felt her children should adopt, and the document soon became a living statement of how that family lives honorably in this world.

Remember, your children's input is important—unless they feel they have a role in the development of the final product, they may not be very inclined to adopt its principles. You may need diplomatically to remind them from time to time, though, that families are not democracies, and this is not a one person, one vote circumstance. Their input is valued, but when it comes to health and safety, you have veto power.

2.11 You are the Most Powerful Role Model

James A. Baldwin said it best when he wrote, "Children have never been very good at listening to their elders, but they have never failed to imitate them." This is a scary thought—you are always being watched! Your actions, both good and bad, will ultimately be mimicked by your children. Parents who smoke automatically ensure that their children are more likely to smoke also.[xxiii] On the other hand, Jonathan is a voracious reader, and our 9-year-old daughter is a reading maniac. The point is that everything we do is a message, a how-to manual for our children. If you dart in and out of the carpool lane without regard for the double yellow line, you may get to your destination a few minutes earlier, but you will also teach your children that rules can be broken if they are inconvenient or frustrating. If you drink every time you socialize, you may end up teaching your children that they have to drink in order to have fun.

This does not mean you can't drink—it means you have to be aware of patterns. Occasional, moderate alcohol use that isn't immediately followed by driving is a relatively benign way for non-addicted adults to inject a little fun into a social situation, but if you always socialize by using alcohol it's possible your children will learn the lesson we talked about earlier, "I need alcohol to have fun and be social." If you drink, you don't need to stop in order to protect your children, but you should teach them moderation by behaving moderately. Remember, though, some things that can be done relatively safely by adults can't be done safely, even when done moderately, by children or teenagers. You are always being watched. This will either benefit your children or harm them; it's your choice. If your actions lack awareness, we suspect the outcome will be much less positive.

2.12 Discuss the Consequences of Use Before it Occurs

If there is one aspect of drug discussions that elicits an almost universal agreement by drug educators and counselors, it is that the consequences for drug and alcohol use should be clearly outlined before the use occurs.[xxiv] This is not an attempt on your part to say, "I fully expect you will use, and here's what's going to happen when you do." This is much more an effort to say, "I hope and expect you will honor our family values and not use, but I understand you live in a world where some people do use. If you choose to be one of those people, here is what it will cost you." Please don't predispose your children to the use of drugs and alcohol by expecting that it will happen. Remember, not all kids do drugs.

Unfortunately, today's use statistics insist that some kids are going to use. No parent wants his or her child to use, and yet someone's child will. It may be yours. By discussing the consequences of use before it happens, you are accomplishing a number of goals:

1. You allow your child to factor in the cost of an action, in exactly the same way we discussed in the curfew section. Of course, you can't establish an exact punishment for an act that has yet to occur, but you can create a menu from which to choose. The typical punishment will entail the pain of loss—what your child values most will define the nature of the punishment. The general areas are pretty universal—cell phones, iPods, cars, drivers' licenses, social events, musical instruments, sports

activities, freedom—anything a child values is on the table as a consequence of use.

As always, the punishment should fit the crime. If your child is a sober attendee of a party where drinking and drug use are taking place, that's one thing. That same child drunk or high at the party is another thing entirely. If your child was the host who provided the drugs and alcohol for the party, that's a completely different ballgame. Each instance calls for a different degree of consequence.

We're not going to explore the philosophy of punishment and its effectiveness here; rather we'll choose to accept as the norm that parents usually use punishment to motivate change in the face of undesirable or unsafe behaviors. Some people suggest, though, that punishment should not just be about taking away more and more of your kids' stuff until they acquiesce. We have heard the suggestion that punishment should be used to get children more involved with activities that will teach them a lesson about the nature of their behavior. Maybe children caught drinking or using drugs should spend some time doing volunteer work at a drug rehab where kids like them are trying to get clean and sober. Children caught drinking and driving might learn something valuable at a meeting where parents speak of the loss of their beloved child or spouse at the hands of a drunk driver; or they could spend a few weekends handing out literature at a DUI checkpoint. We're not advocating one form of punishment over another, just suggesting that punishment can take many forms.

Finally, it should go without saying (that was a joke, by the way) that it is never appropriate to punish children physically or torture them emotionally in an effort to make them behave.

2. When you discuss the consequences of use with your children, you give them a believable way to deflect the offer of drugs or alcohol. One of the hardest things teens will ever do is say no to something other people are doing and not lose their friends. It's hard to maintain social status if someone is calling you a baby or a wimp. If your child can look another in the eye and say, "Really, I can't—if I get caught doing that my mom will saw my leg off with a butter knife," then maybe you have just averted a potential disaster. The declaration, "If I get caught I won't be able to get my license," has saved many young people from using.

We want to make one important note about negative consequences and punishment—make sure your stated consequences are not just empty threats. If you say you're going to do something, you have to do it! You will immediately lose most of your power and legitimacy if you impose a punishment and then let it slide after the first day. Many of our students know their parents are paper tigers. More than once, we've heard kids say something like, "Yeah, they talk a lot, but they'll never stick with it." It's not just a matter of not living up to your word, either. When you threaten a punishment and then don't follow through, you are also making a statement that's loud and clear: "I don't really think this topic is as important as I said it is."

51

Your kids will naturally reason that if it really mattered, you would have cared enough to follow up.

3. When you discuss the consequences of use with your children, you also open the door to discuss with them the consequences of not using. This allows you the opportunity to change behavior in a much more positive way, and we feel this is a much more proactive way to deal with the drug and alcohol issue in your family.

2.13 Teach Your Children to Set Goals

We feel it's only fair that if you're going to punish use, you should reward non-use. One of the basic tenets of motivating people says you get better results by reinforcing desired behaviors than you do punishing undesired ones. One of Jonathan's old management trainers used to say, "You've got to catch them doing something right!" If you can arrange it so you can catch your child doing something right, you can reinforce that behavior by rewarding it. Many people create this circumstance by teaching their child to set goals. Start young if you can, start simply when you do, and base rewards on what your values tell you is appropriate.

A few things about goals: they should be clear, they should be written down, and they should have an end—a point where success can be measured. Once a goal is met and rewarded, a new goal is set.

For years, we've told the story of a mom and daughter who told us about their system. The goal was for the daughter to not drink or use drugs. The period was six months. The reward was two tickets to the concert of the daughter's choice—one ticket for her, one for a friend to go with her. Every six months, the mom and daughter would have an earnest discussion about whether the goal had been met. If it was determined that it had, the tickets were hers. If they ever determined that she had used, the daughter would have to go to school for an entire year without makeup. OK—going to school without makeup is not an earth-shattering consequence for most people, but to this young woman it was massive—this was something that really mattered to her! We knew this family for a number of years, and to the best of our knowledge, the daughter never did use.

Some parents have expressed concern about a system where a child's cooperation is up for sale. That's a valid point, but that's not what we're suggesting. The reward can take any form, some material, some more ethereal. Maybe the reward is a statement of your honest appreciation of your child's character, maybe it's a new right or privilege your child wants. Whatever form it takes, we think goal setting is a huge tool—we think you should use it.

2.14 Help Your Children Achieve Their Goals

When it comes to goals about resisting drug and alcohol use, Ronald Reagan's three words come to mind: "Trust, but verify." We are not claiming that your children aren't trustworthy; but this isn't about trust—it's about health and safety. All teenagers can be trusted on one level or another; it's just that you, as a parent, have to realize that trust has to be limited to areas where your teens have exhibited competence. Of course, they can't become competent without practice, but practice and skill development have to be structured so your children can accomplish them without harming themselves or others. You can probably trust your thirteen-year-old son to wash your car, but you would be a fool to trust that he safely and competently could drive that same car to the carwash.

On the issue of trust, though, most parents would agree that teenagers, as a species, are relatively impulsive and unpredictable. It's not that they're untrustworthy as a measure of character; it's that they don't have the life experience, brain maturity, and skill set required to make good choices when challenged by temptation. The best-laid plans will go out the door in a second if a socially powerful peer suggests something and everyone else immediately adopts that as the new plan. Here are a few things you can do to help your children meet their goals:

1. **Greet them when they come home from a night out.** You don't have to lurk in the front hall and scare them witless as they

come in, but you should have a five minute conversation with your children immediately upon their return home from a night out socializing with their friends (or even if they were out on their own). Some moms recommend the "hug and sniff" greeting, and that's good as far as it goes, but just a few minutes of conversation is so powerful. First, it sets a baseline for normal behavior. If your son or daughter isn't usually drunk or high when they come home, but then one night they are, you'll probably hit on the change fast. If your children know you'll be sitting there when they get home, they are much less likely to be completely polluted when they do. Greeting your children at the door isn't something that should begin when they are teenagers-- start early and be consistent.

As your children get older, their curfew may actually be after your bedtime. In that case, don't let them find you lolling in a puddle of your own drool at the kitchen table, and you can't really go to bed and expect they'll wake you when they get home. It's hard to tell the next morning if they really did forget or if there was a more nefarious reason for the lapse. Instead, here's the foolproof solution to the curfew vs. bedtime dilemma:

2. ***You* sleep in *their* bed.** When they get home, their first job is to wake you up and get you out of their bed. This simple effort ensures that you will get your 5 minutes of conversation, no matter how late their curfew is. If you have a teenage son, he may be kind of creeped out by the notion of you sleeping in his

bed (not to mention how you feel about it!), and if that's the case, just do what one junior boy told his mom when she laid out the plan, "Bring a sleeping bag."

The mother who taught us this said it started out as a police action, but ultimately it became the best parenting she ever did. As she described it, most of the time her daughter would wake her up and quickly report on the utter sameness of her evening out. On a few occasions each year, though, her daughter would glow with the excitement of something wonderful that had happened. But every once in a while her daughter would share with her something terrible that had happened—her heart had been broken, or she had witnessed something awful, and right when her daughter needed her the most, there she was. One of the most important roles a parent can play is that of a shoulder to cry on; but if you miss the immediacy of the moment, it will probably be lost. The feelings won't be dealt with by sharing them; by morning, they may just be buried.

3. **Call ahead.** When your children want to attend a party at another person's home, it really is your duty to call ahead and find a few things out. These calls aren't required for 6-year-old birthday parties, but you might want to start the call-ahead pattern early so your children are trained to expect it when they reach their teens. The purpose of calling ahead is to find out the nature of the event. Most people will open the call with

something like, "I understand your child is having a party, and I just wanted to know if there's anything I can do to help." If the response is, "Party?" you can be sure this is not a good situation—the parents of the host student aren't even aware the party is happening. If the answer is more along the lines of, "Thanks so much, but we're fine," at least you know the parents are aware of the party's existence. From about the 8th or 9th grade on, your calls should include a few more questions:

a. Will you be home for the entire evening?

b. Will adult supervision be present and adequate?

c. Will you be allowing alcohol or other drugs to be used or present? (Really, you do have to ask this.)

d. Will you be allowing young people to leave the party and then return? (Party safety 101 says once a young person is in, they can't leave unless they intend to leave for good.)

e. Will you call me if you have any concerns or problems with my child's behavior? (Wouldn't you rather know earlier rather than later if there are issues?)

If they haven't hung up on you or asked you heatedly what kind of person you think they are, and you are satisfied with their answers, you can be sure your child will be safe at their party. If you've done your due diligence and you already know your kid's friend's parents, you won't have to make this kind of detailed call each time—just ring them up and ask the "Can I help" question and be done with it.

If the parent is unknown to you, though, you have to make the call. One thing that makes these calls so hard is that so few people actually do it. If more people called ahead, we'd all get more practice at making and receiving them gracefully when they are necessary. We've seen over the years that the norm is not to make the call. Parents regularly report to us that they've recently had a party at their home, and if 30 students and friends attend, usually only two or three parents will call ahead. If more parents called ahead, a lot of heartache could be easily avoided.

4. **Occasionally go into the parties your children are attending.** Yes, your children are going to die of embarrassment, but do it anyway. You might want to go in when you drop your children off (give them a 5 minute head start if you want to give them a break, but assure them you'll be looking for them immediately if things don't check out), but when they get older it will behoove you to occasionally drop in when the party is well underway. Many parents we meet hope, or naively assume, that drugs and alcohol aren't present at the parties their children attend. If they're right, great, no problem; but if they're wrong, they really owe it to themselves to check it out.

5. **Have a code word.** The possibility exists that your children might find themselves in a bad spot. They may need your help

getting out of it, but they just can't be seen calling mommy or daddy when things get hairy. If you have a pre-arranged code word that alerts you to your child's situation, you can arrange for their rescue without them having directly to ask you. A few things have to happen first for this to work:

a. They have to start calling you on an arranged schedule when they are out with their friends. The younger you start this, the easier it will be to make it a habit. Every hour, every 90 minutes, every 2 hours; whatever you agree on, they have to call you at the appointed hour. You aren't just training your children here—you're training their friends. If their friends all know your kids have to make the call, they won't see anything unusual when the situation arises that prompts your children to use the code word.

b. When they use the code word, go get them. Don't make them explain why they need you—that's why you have the code word!

c. Plan and role-play what it is that you'll say to get them out of there ASAP. Maybe you can say someone is sick and you need their help, maybe you can say their grandmother died again, maybe you just start yelling for no reason so your children can hold the phone up and complain, "Will you listen to this harpy? I gotta go, you guys." Whatever you agree is going to be said, it needs to be designed to get them out.

d. If your children are calling you because they're drunk or high, go get them—but don't use the "no questions asked" promise we hear about so often. Of course you're going to ask questions—it's your job! Everyone who works in this field agrees, though, that you don't discuss actions or consequences with children who are drunk or high. They won't remember what was said, it's highly unlikely you'll get any sense out of them anyway, and, most importantly, you're going to be angry and scared and emotional—now isn't the time to be making decisions or proclamations about what's going to happen. If you've already discussed the consequences of use with your children, you really don't need to talk to them about what's going to happen—that job is already done. Get them to bed, and deal with the rest in the morning.

We don't think you should spend a lot of energy worrying that your children won't call you if you insist on consequences for use. When you have the consequences talk, assure them as earnestly as possible that they are the most important thing in the world to you—you will always save them. Continue, though, that it is because you love them so much that you can't let something as devastating as drug and alcohol use pass without comment or consequence. (Maybe you can bend a little, but don't do it until after the fact. If your children made a mistake, but after making the mistake they reached out for help, maybe the good judgment they

61

showed by reaching out to you should be rewarded with a mitigation of the severity of the consequence. If they did the right thing in the end, it could make sense to ease up a little on the cost of their earlier poor judgment.) If you have agreed to a No Questions Asked policy, then you may have missed the opportunity to have a meaningful discussion about lessons that can be learned from big mistakes.

6. **Do your children a favor—take their cell phones away when they go to bed.** Here's one thing you can be sure of—no good can come of a text message or a call on your child's cell phone after midnight. Just put the charger in your room, and each night the phone should find its way to the charger before your child goes to bed. Your kids are masters at networking, but they don't need to network at 1:00 a.m.

2.15   The One Question Your Kids Will Always Ask

One question will always be asked if time constraints prevent us from covering it in the parent presentation — "What should I say if my kids ask me about my drug use?" Before we answer, let's go over a few basics. First, there is no universally accepted answer to this question. Some very smart, very accomplished people who work in our field disagree with our take on the issue. Second, lying is not an option, in our opinion. If you are going to lie when your kids hit you with hard questions, you're going to expend a huge amount of energy just keeping your story straight. If your kids do catch you in a lie, you're going to do untold damage to your relationship. By the way, lying won't work over time anyway. You might not realize it, but if you used to use drugs when you were younger, there are probably dozens of evidence bombs lurking in your attic and closets. We always tell parents, "If there's a picture of you in a tie-dyed t-shirt, wearing granny glasses, with The Who on stage in the background—you've smoked some dope! (If you're younger than us, insert the appropriate era's fashion and music, but the final point will be the same—you're caught!)

If you used to use drugs and want to lie to your kids about it, you have to burn all your high school yearbooks, burn all the love letters you kept, cease allowing high school and college friends to visit, and sever all ties to your family. Each of these will at some point or another put truth to your lie, and then it's game over. You have shown you are willing to manipulate your children with lies in order to make them do what you want them to do.

However, if you're not going to lie, what should you do? Some people insist you should just not answer the question. We've heard speakers suggest that you should say, "This isn't about me—we're talking about you." Sorry, we think this non-answer is an answer just the same, but it's an answer without the opportunity for discussion. The non-answer advocates insist that a parent who admits drug use has in essence placed a bar that the child is now obligated to jump over. We think there's a problem, though—when a person refuses to answer, which way do you think the child will lean—toward a presumption of guilt, or one of innocence?

Therefore, you can't lie, and you can't refuse to answer, so that leaves just one option—answer. We believe that you should answer, but you have to answer exactly the right way. Here are some precautions you need to think about before you answer, though:

1. Don't answer if your children are not emotionally ready for the truth. If they're too young, just distract them. "Is that an eagle!?" usually works in our house.

2. Don't answer the question until it's asked.

3. If you're answering an older child's query, remember that the younger children will soon hear a replay unless you discuss this concern with the older child as a part of your answer.

4. Make sure you understand that, for this to work, you cannot currently be abusing legal drugs or using illegal drugs at all.

When You Do Answer, Use This 3 Step Outline As A Guide:

1. Your first sentence is, "Yes, I did." Did you notice the period at the end of that sentence? Don't go into graphic details about your drug use—no laundry lists of drugs you did, no party stories that might serve only to glorify your past use.

2. Your second effort should put your use into context. You are not trying to make excuses here; rather you're trying to explain the climate in which your use occurred. If you're Jonathan's peer, you didn't even have drug education in school—it just didn't exist back then. In addition, many of the drugs of abuse weren't even illegal back then. LSD wasn't illegal until 1966, ecstasy wasn't banned until 1985, and the date-rape drug GHB wasn't outlawed until 1997. Obviously, legal status doesn't make a drug safe or not safe, but legality goes a long way when explaining the context in which your drug use occurred. Here is one of the few times when pleading ignorance can be a positive—we really didn't know what we were doing! Another point to make here is that the nature of drugs has changed over the years—the dangers of drugs are better understood today, drugs are more widely available, and they are purer and stronger than they used to be. This whole effort should not last more than a minute.

3. Your third point should sum up why you stopped. It isn't necessary to make things up, just think about how you came to your non-use position. Many people say they stopped because they just got bored, or that the promise drugs initially held had

proved empty. Others say they stopped when they contemplated the idea of having children. It's hard to be high and be a good parent; the two seem exclusive. We like how this last one sounds, too—"I stopped because I had you, and I only wanted to give you my best." If it's true, it's a powerful thing to be able to say to your kids.

At the end of your answer, one of two things will probably happen—one, your children will be fine with what you've said and that will be the end of it, or two, your children will insist that since you got to learn through experience, they should have the same right and opportunity. If you find yourself confronted by an experiential learner, we think the best answer we've ever heard came from a letter written by a headmaster back east. The points expressed in the letter came to us via conversation, so we can't even give credit to the author, but their wisdom is too dear to pass up. In a letter to the parent body on the subject of experiential learners, which we'll paraphrase here, he said, "There are lots of things you don't have to take part in to know they are bad. You don't have to be a racist to know that racism is evil. You don't have to take part in genocide to know it's against the laws of God. You don't have to use drugs to know they are harmful--I'm here to tell you that." We think it's the best answer we've heard. It's earnest, it's honest, and it's to the point.

One last point about questions concerning your use: don't let your lack of prior experience convince you that you can't adequately help your kids avoid drug and alcohol use. Parents constantly approach us with, "I never used drugs. I don't know how I can help my kids when it comes to drugs." This one kills us every time! We want to say, "Do you hear yourself? You never used! You're the perfect person to teach your child how not to use drugs! You're the role model!" It seems we're are still stuck with the notion that the kids who drank, used, and partied were the "cool" kids; that they were popular and the non-users were nerds. Seriously, it's time to get over it! First, geek is the new cool—you have now officially grown into being cool. Second, the popularity of users, and their prevalence, is overstated. There are actually fewer users than most kids imagine, and, if you think about it, *all* of today's addicts and alcoholics came from the ranks of those who used—it's a requirement. It's time to stop thinking of yourself as a loser just because you didn't party in high school and college.

The other side of this last point is this—you are not a hypocrite if you used to use but you don't want your kids to. If you still use illegal drugs or abuse legal ones and you don't want your kids to, yes, you are a hypocrite. If you used to use, stopped, and now don't want your kids to use, you aren't a hypocrite—you're a teacher.

2.16 Monitor Internet Use in Your Home

This is not the forum for in-depth discussions on internet safety, but we want to go over a few cautions. We think internet connections represent a portal into a world of information that is unparalleled in our history, and yet because that information base is so vast it is both helpful and harmful at the same time. A child doing a keyword search on a drug term will be exposed to a massive array of drug information. Unfortunately, the majority of it will be about how to use the drug, how to get it, how to get around drug tests for it, how to manufacture it, and how anyone who says drugs are harmful is a liar or a puritan.

Please take the time to monitor your child's internet use. A lot of new information shows that kids are good at steering clear of the most dangerous aspects of the internet, but we need to maintain a watchful eye over what they see there.

2.17 Medicine Chests and Liquor Cabinets

The Partnership for a Drug Free America says one of every five teens has abused prescription drugs.[xxv] The NIH says 20% of people in the US have used prescription drugs for non-medical reasons.[xxvi] The year 2006 was the first year where a child who decided to use drugs for the first time was more likely to abuse prescription drugs than they were to smoke marijuana.[xxvii] Prescription drugs like Vicodin, OxyContin, Valium, Ritalin and Adderall are growing in popularity every year, and it's time to wake up.[xxviii] Your medicine chest, if it contains any drug that might be abused, is a danger zone. Prescription drugs that can be abused don't belong in a place that is open and unsupervised. Drugs that can be abused belong under lock and key—that's the way the pharmacy treats them, why should our homes be any different?

Most parents wouldn't suspect that their children would be taking and abusing prescription drugs from home, but it really isn't just about your kids. What about the friends that visit (and this includes your friends); are you sure about all of them? It's like the old saw—strong locks keep people honest. You are the second or third most likely source of prescription medicines that are abused by teens.[xxix] You can help stop the flow of prescription drugs into your child's world by doing this very simple thing—take the drugs with abuse potential out of your medicine chest and secure them.

While we're on the subject, we should also note that over the counter (OTC) drugs are also potential sources of abuse. Most cold medications contain dextromethorphan (DXM) which can cause a high when taken in large doses. On January 1, 2012, California became one of the first states to limit the sale of medications containing DXM to those under the age of 18 without a prescription. Stimulant drugs like caffeine and ephedrine can be found in cold, sinus or diet pills. Even though these OTC drugs are legal and available, they can be dangerous or fatal when abused. Children who take cold medicine before bed when they have a cold are not what we're talking about here, but if you were to find two or three blister packs of Coricidin Cough and Cold (CCC or "skittles") empty in your trash can, you'd have a totally different, and dangerous, situation on your hands. It's time to get aware about the medicines we keep in our homes.

In addition, if you have a bar in your home, or a liquor cabinet, you need to stay on top of your inventory. Teens report that their parents' liquor cabinets and bars are a huge source of alcohol they abuse. If you do drink in your home, you don't have to stop. However, you do need to monitor how much you have in stock. If you had two cases of beer yesterday, but today you only have one, something happened—you had a party, you drank all of it yourself and therefore need to go to rehab, or somebody made off with some of your beer. You need to know where your alcohol is going.

Water and vodka look the same when they're in a vodka bottle. Occasionally, you need to make sure that your clear liquors— vodka, gin, rum, tequila, etc.—are still actually alcohol based liquids and not just water that has been cleverly substituted by your teen.

Taste your clear liquors occasionally, just to be sure. Some parents have tried putting marks on their liquor bottles as a way to keep track of what they have. A restaurateur recently told us a trick about how to mark the amount of liquor in a bottle in a way that might not be so obvious to the casual observer. Instead of marking the bottle as you might normally (with the bottle standing upright), turn the bottle upside down, so the neck is facing downward, then mark the bottle, turn it back over and return it to your liquor cabinet. Many teens will see the mark, but few will figure out this simple system. Again, we do not consider all teens to be evil little trolls that steal and abuse drugs and alcohol. We do, however, hear more stories than we'd care to about teens that get into very dangerous situations that begin with drugs and alcohol obtained in the home.

2.18 One Final Thought

In the face of all this, it's sometimes hard to imagine how we can ever enjoy having kids in our lives, and yet that's what makes all this worth the trouble. Our daughter is the most amazing thing that has ever happened to us. When things get rough, as they are sure to when you love something that is human and flawed and tempestuous and driven by impulse, it pays to remember one thing—the way you felt when that little wonder first entered your life. Jonathan insists his whole world changed the day the nurse put our daughter in his arms for the first time—it was when he learned how to love.

Think back to the first day you laid eyes on your child. What were your intentions that day? What dreams did you dream about what you and your child would become? When times are tough and life gets scary, remember those intentions—they are what give us the strength and the passion to carry on. For carry on we must—it's the job we signed up for; and it's the most important job of all.

Part 3

Some Kids are Going to Use
Drugs and Alcohol

3.1   A Sad Truth: Some Kids are Going to Use

We titled this book *Not All Kids Do Drugs* because we wanted to: (1) dispel the notion that all kids are going to do drugs or drink; and (2) dispense with the idea that using drugs and alcohol constitutes a rite of passage for teens.

If we automatically assume our children are going to use drugs and drink, we almost guarantee that it will happen. Despite outward appearances, our children regularly and passionately try to please us. One of the major reasons cited by teens for not using drugs is that they don't want to disappoint their parents, so we must remember that our expectations play a large part in how our children ultimately behave. What a shame it is when parents give up the fight and expect use on the part of their children. We need to rethink our expectations and reset the default position to non-use.

That said, the idea that not all kids do drugs comes with a companion realization: some kids are going to use. This is a sad but simple fact—a certain percentage of kids are eventually going to drink, do drugs, or both; but it's critical that we quantify this and assure you that while use does happen, it doesn't happen at the rate most parents we talk to assume it does.

3.2 Perspective is Key—What is Actually Happening

At the time of this writing (2012) the most recent statistics available said that about two thirds of all high school seniors drank alcohol at least once during their senior year. By itself, that sounds bad—two out of every three seniors drank in the past year. However, if you look a little deeper, the picture starts to change.

Yes, two of three drank, but the sole qualification to become a part of that statistic was to have consumed a single alcoholic drink in the previous twelve months—that's one 12 ounce beer, 5 ounces of wine, or 1.25-1.5 ounces of distilled spirits like vodka, gin, tequila, etc. So, if some of the kids in that two thirds statistic qualified by drinking one drink, we need to ask another question—how many got drunk in their senior year? Answer: less than half—about 44%.

That's a little better, but still daunting. Half of the seniors in the country were drunk in the past year. As we've said before (and will no doubt repeat numerous times in the coming pages): *it is never safe or healthy for teens to drink or use drugs*. Again, this is an exercise in perspective, so let's ask one final question: how many of these kids got drunk on a regular basis in that year (i.e., at least once per month)? Answer: 27%.

The bad news is that about one quarter of high school seniors in the U.S. got drunk regularly in the past year. The good news is that three quarters of them didn't, and we want to make sure we focus on that. It is critical that we acknowledge that the majority of seniors in high school don't drink on a regular basis, and it's imperative that we change our expectation that all kids are going to drink and use drugs. Imagine what a difference we could make in these statistics if we just stopped expecting that all kids are going to use.

3.3   Your Choice—Are You Proactive or Reactive?

Unfortunately, we still must accept the fact that some kids are going to drink and use drugs; and most of them eventually are going to be caught when they do. Of course, this is one of the nightmares parents dread the most—what are you supposed to do when you catch your child drinking or using drugs? If you are one of the unfortunate parents facing this dilemma, how you handle the situation will play a big part in how it eventually resolves. Whether it is the blow that puts your relationship with your teen on its back— or the opportunity that allows you to develop a deeper communication with your child—depends largely on how you act in the hours, days, and weeks that follow.

It is of the utmost importance that parents realize drug and alcohol use by teens cannot be looked upon as youthful indiscretion. This is not a case of your daughter dating a person with too many tattoos—it is an emergency; and when you first discover your child using drugs or drinking you must act. How you act is the topic of discussion this section is dedicated to; but it needs to be clear that this cannot be overlooked or minimized. The day you find out your child is using drugs or drinking is the day you need to muster every resource in an effort to forestall future use.

In our second book, *The Mother's Checklist of Drug Prevention*, we spend a lot of time discussing the differences between proactive and reactive parenting. Parents who are proactive, who reflect on the future and develop game plans for how they will deal with certain issues, are positioned better than those parents who find themselves poorly prepared. The latter group of parents typically reacts to each new surprise with no plan or idea about what to do and no information about whether or not what they are doing will even work. Sadly, these parents often do exactly the wrong thing and cause a lot more damage than if they had taken more time to formulate their plan. When you parent, a proactive style works better than a reactive one does.

3.4 A Parent's Challenge—React, or Respond?

If you are unfortunate enough to find yourself in the role of the parent that just caught a child doing drugs or drinking, you're going to face two options: (1) you can react, or (2) you can respond; and although these may sound like the same thing, they're not. When you react, you are dealing with a situation the moment it comes up. You don't have a plan, and you haven't put any thought into how you would like this problem to resolve. When you respond, you are following a game plan that you worked out well in advance of the occurrence, and you are staying true to what you believe and what your projected best-case scenario is. There is a huge difference.

As Southern Californians, we equate this situation to one we might find ourselves facing when the proverbial "big one" hits—the earthquake of huge destructive power that will eventually befall us. Proactive people that are lucky enough to survive the initial shock will be able to respond by gathering in their prearranged meeting spots, secure in the knowledge that they will at least have enough food and water to survive the first few days after the initial event. They will be able to do this because they planned and put aside an earthquake kit in preparation for this eventuality.

Reactive people, on the other hand, will be in bad shape. Once the pumps stop, they may have no drinkable water available until tanker trucks arrive or service is restored. Hunger will quickly become a serious issue if the food in their homes is buried under tons of rubble or incinerated in the natural gas-fueled explosions and fires that can follow a quake of large magnitude. Failure to plan for such eventualities can result in costs that are unimaginable until it's too late to change them. If you don't have a plan for dealing with the nightmare, it's hard to escape it.

3.5   No Matter the Circumstances, You're in the Right Place

If you are reading this book in advance of any use on the part of your child, you are proactive and you are formulating your response to an event you hope will never happen, but one you want to be prepared for in case it does. If you are reading this because you just recently caught your child drinking or using drugs, not all is lost. You are definitely in reaction mode, but at least you are reaching out for information on how best handle what you currently face. This event, if it happens, is going to feel just like an earthquake. How you plan and how you respond will play a big part in determining how much of the outcome will be seen as cost and how much will be seen as value. Our hope is that the information that follows will increase the value side of the equation substantially.

3.6   The Plan of Action—What's Covered; in What Order

Any situation where parents must deal with a child that is caught drinking or using drugs will have aspects that are unique to that particular circumstance, but space does not allow us to cover each of them in detail. The parental actions that we will discuss here are suggested methods for dealing with this general situation: you have discovered your child is either in possession of, using, or spending time in the presence of teens that are using drugs and alcohol. Any variations on this general theme can be dealt with in much the same way—the details will vary somewhat, but the responses can be tailored to each situation with very little tweaking.

Now that we've dispensed with the preliminaries, let's proceed. First, we'll list some typical examples of how parents catch their kids with drugs or alcohol; then we'll cover a few responses from the kids who were caught; and finally we'll discuss what you should do in order to make the best of what is one of the worst situations parents can face.

3.7 Possible Scenarios

- You catch your child in possession of drugs or alcohol.
- You find drug paraphernalia (rolling papers, water pipes, rolled up paper money, razor blades, digital scales, etc.) in your child's possession.
- Your child is caught at school using, drinking, under the influence, or in possession.
- You are told by another parent that your child is doing drugs or drinking.
- Your child is caught at a party (by you, another parent, or the police) where drugs and alcohol are present.
- Your child is caught at the same party just mentioned, but they aren't just present, they're using.
- Your child is delivered to your door or arrives home drunk or high after a night out with friends.
- Your child becomes secretive in the extreme; last minute sleepovers crop up; curfews are broken regularly; and you suspect drugs and alcohol may be the cause.
- Your child is arrested for driving drunk.
- Your child is found to be riding with or to have previously ridden with a drunk driver.
- Your child's grades are falling precipitously, and drugs and alcohol are suspected to be the cause.

3.8   Possible Responses by Your Child

- "It's not mine. I'm holding it for a friend."

- "I found it. I was just curious, so I picked it up."

- "This was the first time I ever did it. I'll never do it again."

- "My friend's parents said it was ok, since we wouldn't be driving. They're really cool—they were drinking too."

- "I wasn't doing it. I was watching out for my friend's safety."

- "I was the designated driver. I couldn't leave."

- "Whoever said that is lying. Who are you going to trust—me or some stranger?"

- "Everyone's doing it. Do you want me to be a loser?"

- "I only had one. You do it all the time, why can't I? I'm three inches taller than you are. If anyone shouldn't be drinking, it's you."

Your Response—Short Term

3.9 Keep Your Head, but Don't Ignore the Facts

As impossible as it may seem, do not lose your head. Remember to breathe. Your goal here is to deal with the situation in a manner that will address the issue without ruining your relationship with your child, so try to avoid doing or saying something in the heat of the moment that you can't take back or fix later. Do not fall victim to denial—we know you don't want to think of your child as a drinker or drug user, but if it walks like a duck and quacks like a duck, it's probably a duck. As you deal with the situation, be sure to include your spouse in the process—this should not fall to one parent to handle. If you are divorced, follow your co-parenting agreement to the letter to avoid blame from the other parent and repercussions from the courts. In a perfect world, you will have arranged consequences for this type of behavior well in advance—that way, you won't be creating consequences while you are angry and afraid.

3.10 My Kid is Drunk—Now What?

If you are unfortunate enough to find yourself facing a child that is drunk or high, this is the first rule: ***don't waste time and energy talking to him at that point. You aren't going to get any meaningful work done while he is under the influence, so don't try.***

Make sure you take away all means of communication with the outside world—cell phone, laptop, desktop computer, iPod Touch, iPad, etc. He should not be able to communicate with his friends in an effort to get his story straight before you have a chance to talk to him.

Keep an eye on a child that is totally wasted—you might be angry, but you don't want him aspirating his vomit and dying during the night. Remember that his blood alcohol concentration may continue to climb for a significant period after he arrives home, so even if he appears to be ok, check on him frequently throughout the night. If you have any doubts as to whether he is going to make it through the night—if he is having trouble breathing or you are unable to rouse him—seek medical attention before allowing him to sleep it off. It may be expensive, and it may be embarrassing, but you want to err on the side of caution when it comes to the health and safety of your child.

3.11 Rise and Shine, Darling!

Don't allow him to sleep in the next day. Set your alarm for an early wake up—this is not a time to cater to his comfort and ease. One of the true joys (not!) of drinking is the way it can make you feel the next day. What seemed like such a good idea the night before has the potential to turn into sheer physical torture the next morning—last night's revelry is this morning's hangover. While it is true teens don't tend to suffer hangovers as severely as adults do, it will still be seriously unpleasant to for him to have to face the new day after using the night before; so if you can find a copy of Reveille on iTunes, download it and blast it as loud as you can!

You might go so far as to have a nice plate of runny scrambled eggs waiting for him at the table where you intend to talk. If you can, try to chew with your mouth open and let a little food collect at the corners of your lips. Remember, you are trying to extinguish this behavior, and anything you can do to plant negative associations in your child's mind is fair game. It's not about torture, but it certainly is about discomfort. Forewarned is forearmed, though—you may also want to have a wastebasket or bucket nearby for the possible unpleasantness that can follow a night of drinking.

Cancel all events he has planned for the day—he should not expect to continue as though nothing has happened. This day should stick in his mind for a long time; so games, practices, rehearsals, and—yes, we're going to say it—parties are all off the calendar for the time being.

3.12 What to Say; How to Say It

Open the conversation the next morning with a few general statements about the larger picture. The first thing you want to make clear is that you love him, and because you love him you are willing to do whatever is necessary to ensure his safety, no matter how unpleasant it is for you and how much more energy you have to expend dealing with his mess. Explain that while you will always love him, your love does not exclude occasional and justifiable feelings of disappointment and anger because of decisions he has made.

Tell him how you are feeling—disappointed, angry, afraid, confused—but try to do it in a way that makes him understand that it is the behavior he is exhibiting (not the person he is) that you are having the problem with. When you express your disappointment, try to confine your statements to what are called "I" statements. Say what you feel without resorting to accusations and name-calling. It's fine to say something like, "When you use alcohol at this age, it makes me worry beyond reason." Avoid statements that label your child like, "You're a drunk! It's no wonder I'm a nervous wreck! My son is an alcoholic!"

If you want your kids to respect what you feel in the end, you need to take ownership of your feelings. Yes, they may have done something impulsive, and yes, you're worried, but they didn't make you worry. You decided to worry all on your own. It may seem like a small point, but it will benefit you as you try to have deeper emotional discussions with your teens over the years.

3.13 Now it's Their Turn to Talk; Yours to Listen

When it comes to an explanation of the events that led up to the previous evening's drama, "Nothing happened, you're over-reacting," is not adequate. Ask him to explain the sequence of events that resulted in him sitting in front of you now. Try not to interrupt while he explains, and try to limit your side of the conversation to questions that will fill in any areas where you need more information. It may help to have a pad of paper or some other method of jotting down notes about what is said and what questions you would like to address after he finishes his explanation.

Listen carefully to the vocabulary he uses. While it is not expected that you be completely up to speed on every aspect of drug use and the terms associated with it, try to get a feel for how he speaks and what that might indicate about whether he is new to the game or deeply immersed in it.

Excuses and rationalizations should be treated fairly but firmly. While it may be admirable for your child to make efforts to keep his friends safe by watching out for them or playing the part of designated driver, it should still be made clear that he has violated your family's rules and expectations by willingly spending time in the presence of other teens that are drinking and using drugs. His sobriety, if that is the case, is a point in his favor; but it is not enough to carry the day and get him off the hook. You can honor the fact that he made some good decisions, but at the same time, you have to point out the flaws in the bigger picture.

3.14 The Biggest Lie Ever Told: "It's not mine."

If the conversation you are having has been inspired by you finding your child in possession of drugs, you need to be prepared for what is—hands down—the most ridiculous and yet most frequently used dodge teens try to pull in this situation: "It's not mine. I'm holding it for a friend." Here is the translation of what those words actually mean: "It's mine, but I'm betting you're naïve enough and so blinded by hope and love that you'll grab any lifeline and believe this ridiculous lie."

Occasionally, this topic comes up in classes with Jonathan's older students. When he asks what the first words out of a kid's mouth are when he or she is caught with drugs, the students' response comes in the form of a chorus, "It's not mine!"

Let's be clear here—kids don't ask other kids to hold drugs for them. When Jonathan was using, the last thing anyone would do was give him drugs to hold. Do that, and you were never going to see them again. Conversely, he would have been no more likely to give drugs to a friend "to hold" than he would to give them to his parents "to hold." It doesn't happen. Ninety nine times out of a hundred, the drugs you found on your kid belong to your kid.

3.15   Partial Truths are Still Lies

The only time this old lie comes anywhere close to the truth is in the case where two or more friends pool their resources and buy a specific quantity of drugs together. In that situation, it might be possible for one member of the group to be assigned the duty of holding on to their stash until such time as they all got together to get high, but the point remains—your daughter isn't holding someone else's drugs exclusively, she's holding her drugs and someone else's drugs simultaneously. Despite whatever protestations she trots out, the truth is this: she is in possession of drugs, and they are hers. Any steps you take after this point to deal with the situation should arise from this truth.

In addition, while it may occasionally be possible to find drugs lying around, it is anything but common. Even if it's true and your child did find drugs by accident, that's still no excuse for why she still has them. The idea that your child found drugs only a few moments before you caught her in possession of those drugs is a non-starter. Again, it just doesn't happen like that.

3.16 The First Time Probably isn't the First Time

The other most commonly employed evasive maneuver a kid will use in this situation is to say that while you did catch her doing it this thing this time, it has never happened before. Common sense and probability insist that not all parents catch all kids the first time they use drugs or alcohol, so the chances that "It's the first time I've ever done this" are nowhere near as high as you might hope. In addition, even if it is true, the fact remains you are facing a situation where she was caught possessing, using, or in the presence of drugs or alcohol; and that is a behavior that won't be allowed to continue. The steps you take here are to ensure that this situation won't be repeated.

3.17 Do not be Thankful it's Only...

Please don't fall into the trap of feeling relieved that your kid is using one of the "less dangerous" drugs. It's a cliché when parents utter the words, "Thank God it was only...." Dispense with this type of thinking now—it's not better to catch your kid using alcohol than it is to catch them using some other drug; and marijuana is not the soft little bunny drug that hops around and doesn't hurt anybody. If your teen is using any drug, including and especially alcohol, you have a problem on your hands—a big problem. What we now know about adolescent brain development says that teens can't use drugs and alcohol safely, even in seemingly small or moderate doses.

3.18   Should You Drug Test?

You're going to need to decide if you want to do a drug test or not. If you do, you have to do it that day—you can't wait. When it comes to drug testing, the sooner the test is done the more likely you are to get an accurate representation of what your child has been exposed to over the last 24-72 hours. Any big-name pharmacy chain will have home drug test kits available, and many of these stores are open all night. You probably don't need to waste any money on an alcohol test—if you can smell it on their breath, they are uncoordinated, and they are slurring their words, they're probably drunk.

A drug test can help give you more information to work with in cases where you have already established that your child is using but you don't know exactly what drugs are involved; and more information will allow you to make better decisions about how to proceed. Poly-drug use (concurrent use of two or more drugs at the same time) is quite common, so a drug test will give you a clearer view of what's really going on in your teen's life.

Unfortunately, there are some downsides to drug tests. They are notoriously hard to trust, and they might even come back negative for a kid that actually is using drugs. In addition, they are usually set up as a two-step process—first you do the home test, and if that comes up positive, you send the sample out for further testing by a lab. This can take a good amount of time, and meanwhile you're losing the intensity of the moment.

It is helpful also to remember what's important in this situation. The problem isn't what drugs your kid is doing—the problem is that your kid is doing drugs.

If you do find yourself in a circumstance where drug testing is necessary, as in a situation where you have long suspected your child is using drugs but never seem to be able to catch him or to be sure, arrange for a series of random tests to be conducted at a medical facility. In that case, you can be reasonably confident that what the test indicates is accurate.

We usually advocate drug tests in a couple of limited situations—first, when dealing with oppositional, out-of-control teens who are in serious danger of hurting themselves, or, more proactively, when you and your teen work together and agree that regular drug testing might be the very thing he can use to avoid offers of drugs and alcohol. "I can't you guys—my parents drug test me," can go a long way toward keeping your son away from drug and alcohol use.

The big dilemma parents face when they drug test is that it tends to undermine the most important thing they can do to lessen the chances their kids will use drugs—develop, over time, a lifelong relationship with their children that is based on trust and communication. Unless it is conducted as a team effort on the parts of both parents and their children, drug testing usually indicates an absence of trust and a serious lack of communication. Unless there is an imminent, direct threat to your children's health and safety, we feel your time and energy will be much better spent on efforts to strengthen your relationship with your children. In dire circumstances, though, extreme measures may be called for. In those situations, you do whatever is necessary to protect your children, up to and including drug testing.

Your Response—Long Term

You'll need to discuss what the consequences will be for the behavior your son or daughter has exhibited. For an in-depth exploration of rules, expectations, and consequences, please see our book *Where's the Party?*; but we'll cover the basics here.

3.19 The Biggest Consequence—Friends

We hope you have, at a much earlier time, laid out the consequences for violations of the family's drug and alcohol policies. All is not lost if you haven't, but you are in a less than optimal position due to your lack of preparation. The goal here is to make your child aware that the decision to break family rules about drug and alcohol use will come at a cost, and one of the costs you can implement here can do double duty—contact with friends.

First, the loss of contact with friends is a big price for a kid to pay—her friends mean a lot to her at this age, and losing that contact is a hefty punishment. Second, if the friends we're talking about spend a lot of time with your child, they are more than likely aware of the use that occurred and are also quite likely doing the same things she is doing.

One of the most powerful indications that a kid will do drugs or alcohol is the presence of peers that use as well, so if you limit her access to these friends you have not only punished her, you have also removed one of the major drivers of her use.

Another consequence that does double duty is access to social events—the loss of those social contacts is costly for your child, but that loss also limits her exposure to situations where use has a greater chance of occurring.

3.20 The Goal of Consequences

When the protests start over how unfair your punishments are, remind her that it isn't your fault that these costs have been incurred; these consequences have arisen as a direct result of decisions she made.

This is where your previous ownership of your feelings can start to pay dividends. You feel the way you do about the situation because you have chosen to respond to that circumstance in that way—not because of what your child did to you. In the same exact way, your child is the victim of consequences because of her choices, not because you have some deep-seated need to punish her. She will have to find a way to take responsibility for her actions if she is ever to learn how to control her behavior.

Consequences should be designed to encourage the display of new behaviors and attitudes before they are lessened or removed. Of course, punishments cannot go on forever, but they should carry with them the understanding that your son or daughter has behaved in such a way as to have violated your trust; and he or she must now earn that trust back. You don't want to restrict their social lives forever, but teens should display a certain level of remorse and behavior change if they are to win back their previous curfew times, for example.

3.21 Should You Contact Other Parents?

If your discussions with your children reveal the involvement of any of their friends, we highly recommend you consider contacting the parents of those kids. When you do make these calls, you should be prepared to encounter attitudes about drug and alcohol use that may not be parallel with yours.

You've probably already read enough of this book to realize that many parents still consider drug and alcohol use a normal part of growing up. If that's the case in one of your calls, take it as a plus that you now know your child isn't in the best hands when he's visiting that home. You may want to consider limiting your child's visits to their home to those times when you can be present also; or, if your son wants to spend time with their son, it needs to be at your house from now on. Ultimately, you may be forced to eliminate his exposure to that friend, especially if you suspect that the other child's use is ongoing.

When you contact the parents of any other teens that were involved, you are helping them and yourself in a number of ways. First, you put the other parents on notice that you are not going to take this lightly. It may well be that the other parents are wondering how to deal with the situation appropriately and your earnestness can guide them in their response.

Second, you now have a relationship with those parents based on a common goal—your collective kids not doing this again.

That means they will be watching your kids and you will be watching theirs—you're on the same team.

Finally, calling the parents of any other kids involved will almost certainly cause your child a good deal of embarrassment, and most kids will go a long way to avoid future situations where that might happen again.

3.22   When Other Parents Encourage Use

It can be much more difficult to deal with situations where you know or suspect that other parents are providing or allowing the use of alcohol and drugs in their home. Many parents we talk to indicate that they would simply call the police and let them handle it. Our experience has been that while the police are concerned with and opposed to teen drinking, they have difficulty responding quickly to a party where teens are drinking if they have emergencies that are more pressing on their hands. Their head-on car crash is going to trump your party every time.

Your first responsibility is to take the steps necessary to keep your child out of environments where teen drug and alcohol use is known to occur or suspected to be the norm. As to what should be done about parents that serve alcohol to minors or allow its use in their presence, the situation is murky at the time this book is being published. Social host laws (where the hosts are held responsible, civilly or legally, for what goes on at their parties) are being either created or changed regularly in states across the country.

Since the situation is so fluid, we feel our readers will be best served if we continue to update the status of social host issues on our website: www.milestogodrugeducation.com. The current trend is that this issue will get much more press in the coming months and years; and that same trend seems to indicate that people are becoming more aware and less tolerant of the dangers posed by teen parties where drug and alcohol use is allowed or encouraged. While this may be seen by the parents that host these parties as an invasion of their privacy or a violation of their homes, we see it as good news that has been too long in coming.

At the time of publication of this second edition, we were weeks away from releasing our third book titled *Where's The Party?*, a detailed guide for parents on ways to handle the issues associated with teen parties that feature drug and alcohol use. We are hopeful this new book will aid in speeding the arrival of the day when parents that host these parties will be seen for what they are: immature, irresponsible, and ill informed.

3.23 What's Next—How to Turn This in Your Favor

Discuss with your child the steps you're going to take to ensure his drug and alcohol use doesn't happen again. This is really two things—a new set of expectations and a new set of goals.

The new expectations should make it clear that for the near future he will have to show that the social situations he will be exposed to include adequate amounts of appropriate adult supervision. It is his job to prove this to you, not your job to do all the legwork involved. He needs to provide you with sufficient information—at a minimum, the name, address, and phone number of the supervising adults, so you can check out whether the circumstances will allow for his safe participation.

He will also have to prove to you that he will be where he says he's going to be, and he will have to show you he can work within the limits of whatever you both decide his curfew will be. Of course, these restrictions can be eased as he shows you more responsibility.

That brings us to the second part of this discussion: goal setting. One result of all this turmoil should be a commitment on your child's part that this isn't going to happen again—he should make it a goal he is trying to achieve. One of the basics of goal setting is that the goal should be celebrated when it is achieved. This can take many forms, but in this case one of the rewards for showing increased responsibility can be increased freedom—it becomes a way for him to earn back the trust he lost when he started this mess.

Be very clear in your new rules and expectations, but also be very open to the idea that he can show you a new level of responsibility. It is your job to notice and respond positively to this newfound attitude adjustment. Remember, kids do better when they are complimented for doing something right than they do when being taken to task for doing something wrong. The idea is to use this opportunity to strengthen the bonds you have with your child, not weaken them. While there is usually a lot of emotional turmoil that goes along with situations like these, over time families often look back on them as some of the most important stages in the long process of growing up.

Be sure to take advantage of any opportunities you see to remind your child why all this is happening: because you love him and want only the best for him. You can expect this will be greeted with a lot of eye rolling and the occasional, "Yeah, right—you've got a funny way of showing it," but hold on to the belief that, in the long run, doing the right thing will eventually be rewarded much more generously than taking the easy way out will.

3.24   What if it's Bigger Than You Can Handle?

If catching your child with drugs and alcohol leads you to the conclusion that the problem is bigger than you can handle on your own, you have to be willing to reach out and ask for help. You will have to start assembling the team that will bring your child back to a non-using lifestyle—family, therapists, trusted members of the school community, clergy, and medical professionals can all play a powerful role in getting your child clean and sober again

In the case of deep-seated and ongoing drug use, you will probably want to enlist the services of an assessment professional—someone who can determine the depth of use that now exists. You may need to place your child in drug treatment or get him involved in a support program designed to aid his attempts to stop using. A good place for information and referrals is our website: www.milestogodrugeducation.com.

If you find yourself in a situation where drug and alcohol use is making your child violent, you may even need to involve the police in order to keep you and the rest of your family safe.

Obviously, these are worst-case scenarios, but one thing we've learned over the years is that drugs and alcohol have the potential to take the best people to the darkest places. It doesn't happen to everyone, it doesn't even happen to most, but everyone it happens to has one thing in common—they never thought it would come to this. If it does, you have to act; you can't just sit around hoping it will get better.

The goal here is the same as it is in all the other situations we've just discussed—to help your child be safe; to give him every opportunity to grow up to be a productive, functional adult. There's a lot better chance of that happening if drugs and alcohol, when found to be present, are dealt with in such a way as to end their use. What you want at the end of all this is what you started with: a child that doesn't use drugs or alcohol. While unpleasant, it may be one of the most important and rewarding duties you perform as a parent.

Part 4

How Did You Become the Drug Guys?

4.1 Kelly's Story: I am a drug addict magnet. I am the spouse, friend, family member and colleague of many alcoholics and drug addicts. Not just a few—a lot! My awareness of addiction began when I was in elementary school, but my understanding of it came when I was a teenager. Because I have so many people in my life who are in recovery, I must respect their anonymity. For that reason, I will not be describing my life the way that a recovering alcoholic/addict would do in an autobiography, but I can tell you about how it affected me.

When I was 19, I decided to get my Ph.D. and work with friends and family members of addicts. After having several people in my life who were forever changed by their addiction, I realized that my life was changed by the experience as well. From my perspective, when they needed help, I was the one who cleaned up the mess. I was the one who picked people up when they fell down, held people's hair while they vomited, comforted them and listened to endless babble about their life problems. They all seem to find me eventually. I got to the point where I just wanted to hide.

After a couple of years of college psychology classes, I started realizing that I was a big part of the problem. Attending Al-Anon and Alateen meetings helped explain the impact that these people and their behaviors were having on my life. While I wasn't an addict myself, I was willing to try several drugs and unfortunately liked several of them. Alcohol was not for me, I had a very low tolerance for drinking. It made me sick and I hated that out of control, sleepy feeling.

Nevertheless, since drugs and alcohol were such a prevalent part of the culture in the 70's and 80's, it was easy to copy my friends' behaviors when they started using drugs. Since I had no drug education at all, what I now see as common sense non-use decisions were not so clear to me back then. As a sickly kid and only child, I craved attention from my peers. I am the perfect example of the naïve lamb heading for the slaughter. These are the kids I watch for today that I label the "followers."

Each person experiences drugs in their own way, and some drugs were more attractive to me than others were. I have dyslexia and ADHD, but at that time, I was still undiagnosed. I am so hyperactive (or "naturally caffeinated" as I tell my students) that I found myself attracted to prescription and over the counter drugs that would give me clarity and focus or help me sleep at night. I also regularly sought relief, via the use of prescription and OTC drugs, from the pain of a previous back injury. I was self-medicating, but it wasn't until much later that I learned what that meant. Fortunately, I was the type of person that was able to say, "I don't like what this is doing to my life," and so I stopped before it got completely out of control. My common sense finally kicked in.

In the early 80's, I watched as more and more people around me destroyed themselves with drugs and alcohol, and by the time I was 22 years old I had witnessed several suicide attempts by people close to me. I got scared and decided to abstain from alcohol entirely, which I did for years. Finally, after a few years of school, I realized that I had no desire to spend the rest of my working life listening to people's problems as a psychologist.

At that point, I changed course, went to film/theater school, and fell in love with comedy. I had always been a big fan of Bill Cosby and Bob Newhart, and I thought their jobs looked like a lot more fun than my original career track. I guess the joke was kind of on me when Newhart went on to do such brilliant comedy as a psychologist in "The Bob Newhart Show." I spent the next 10 years working in television, theater and comedy clubs. In the early 90's, I was rushing madly from film school at UCLA to the set of Full House at Sony Studios to the Groundlings on Melrose to the Laff Stop in Newport Beach.

I loved it, and met dozens of goal oriented, focused people who were following their passion, but it struck me as odd that a disproportionate number of the performers were smokers, alcoholics, and addicts. It seemed like most of the funniest performers were cast from the same mold—depressed, self-deprecating, observational comics with very real alcohol and drug habits. This is when my eyes were really opened about the level of depression and addiction that enveloped the performers. However, it wasn't just the performers—the writers were self-loathing and frustrated that their talents were not being rewarded with fame and opportunity, and the aspiring directors and producers seemed convinced they had to play the party scene to make deals. I was constantly dealing with drunks and smokers; not just on the stage, but in the audience as well. I was annoyed and frustrated.

Then, in January of 1992, I lost my home, my pets and all of my belongings in a fire caused by a faulty extension cord. Haunted by loss and heartbreak, I decided to leave California and take a job at a comedy club in Harvard Square in Cambridge. After a year of being in the coldest place I'd ever been in my life, a friend of mine said that she knew a comic that I should meet, because she thought we would have a lot in common. I had just opened my own comedy club, and was attempting to do something special with one-person shows. My first response was "NO, I don't date the comics!" It was the cardinal rule that Cindy Stewart, my good friend and long time manager of another comedy club taught me—don't date the talent! My friend finally wore me down and convinced me I should give this guy a chance. When I first saw Jonathan, my immediate thought was that he was too tall for me (I'm 5'1" and he's 6'2"), but I spoke with him briefly. We eventually met again at an event at the Hard Rock Café in Boston, and I said, "Yes" to dinner.

On our 6 hour dinner date, we told each other our stories. I'm sure he was thinking that I had an enormous amount of baggage, and I certainly thought, "Well, this guy is totally screwed up!" As I listened to his story, though, I realized we had more in common than I originally thought. By the end of our date, I found myself hoping we would see each other again—we had a lot to talk about! Yes, we did go on another date, and we have now been talking for over 15 years; first as a couple, then as business partners, then husband and wife, and finally as parents.

After one year of dating, Jonathan left on tour with a non-profit speakers program talking to kids about drug addiction. I closed the club at the end of the comedy boom and went on tour with Jesus Christ Superstar. As we rolled past the interminable cornfields that bus tours must suffer, Carl Anderson (the original Judas) told me daily that I should take what I knew and start my own lecture series with Jonathan. As the tour was ending, I approached Jonathan with the idea. In typical addict fashion, he was convinced it would never work, but as you can see, my wisdom prevailed!

4.2 Jonathan's Story: My mom and dad were classic examples of parents in the 50's and 60's—dedicated, hard working, and willing to sacrifice personal needs and wants so their kids would have every possible advantage. My dad is the classic stand-up military officer. He's honest, he believes in honor and country, and he's never once abused alcohol or drugs. For most of my early years, my mom was the best friend I had. My favorite times with her were when company was coming over, and I was my mom's helper in the kitchen. She really valued the contributions I was making so her party would be a success, and we enjoyed each other's company immensely. Over the years, she became a seriously gifted artist; she could make friends with just about anyone; and she was downright funny when she wanted to be. The saddest day I've ever had in my life was the day she died.

When we were young, our family went on vacation each year to this idyllic campground on the shores of Long Lake in Maine. On the way, we spent lots of time with extended family. We regularly saw cousins, aunts, uncles and grandparents. I think that out of 1,000 people, 999 of them would have come out of the experience happy, healthy, and well adjusted. I didn't.

I don't remember the first few times our family had to move, but I do remember that we moved excessively because of my father's career as a high-ranking naval officer in the nuclear submarine service. I was always the new kid in class, friends were something you lost, and permanence was an illusion. My dad's service required that he be away for extended periods; he was home for three months and then gone for three months. This alternating absence went on for many years as we were growing up. While he was gone, my mom was left with the job of raising four sons and a daughter by herself.

As I said, my mom was funny, artistic and caring, but she was a victim of her time—a lot of military wives of the day did as they were told, kept their complaints to themselves, took diet pills to look good, took sleeping pills to counter the diet pills, and drank to deal with the pressure. In her later years, my mom's drinking became more of an issue. We didn't appreciate it at the time, but problems with alcohol had plagued her family for generations.

The first emotion I remember feeling was fear, and that was followed closely by loneliness. I was terrified to be left alone in a strange new setting, be it school or summer camp. My relationships were fleeting, my role models were inadequate or absent, and my heart was broken. My dad was a tough disciplinarian; my older brother became a troubled bully of a kid. We, in turn, weren't kind to our younger brothers when it came to name calling and beatings.

In light of all this, my first drug experience seems a foregone conclusion. I was in third grade, the new kid in class, and desperate to be liked and accepted by the cool kids. The coolest kid in our third grade class was this person named Clifford. Now, Clifford was that guy who had been left back a few times already, and he was much older than the rest of the class. He was bigger and tougher than any other third grade boy, and most of the fourth graders for that matter. One day after school, Clifford said to me, "We're going over to my house to smoke cigarettes—you want to come?" In about a second, I did all the calculations. If I was caught, my parents would be livid and the punishment would be mighty. If I said, "No," I would be a baby in the eyes of the boys I was so desperate to impress. If I said, "Yes," the other boys in the class would know I was one of Clifford's smoking gang, and I would be granted the status associated with that position. To me, this was a no-brainer—I was going to smoke cigarettes in Clifford's garage.

My memories of my first cigarette are still clear—it was horrific. The smoke burned my throat, sinuses, and lungs. My eyes watered, I was so dizzy I thought I would fall down, and my stomach was doing flip-flops. My hands shook and I was pouring sweat. The taste in my mouth was so awful all I wanted to do was spit, but we were in Clifford's garage, so I just kept swallowing the nauseating saliva I was producing in such copious quantities. In all, it was the worst thing I had ever purposely done to myself, and yet in my eyes it was so worth it. I got to be a part of something I so desperately wanted—these guys acted like I was their friend. As a group, we mercilessly teased the one guy who changed his mind and wouldn't smoke. Finally, I wasn't the target of the barbs—I was the one delivering them. Smoking, as nasty as it was, made me a part of a peer group. Smoking socialized me when nothing in my almost nonexistent skill set did. Smoking fixed me.

Of course, I was caught, and I was punished. I don't remember the specific consequence, but it really didn't matter— what I got from smoking was so much more valuable to me than any price I had to pay. I felt guilty about the difficulty I caused my parents. Guilt was a constant co-morbid condition with the ever-present fear and loneliness, but at least I could push my feelings out of my head for a little while when I was with those guys and smoking like they were.

The next couple of drugs I used, alcohol and marijuana, followed pretty much the same pattern. I drank alcohol for the first time at the age of 12 in an effort to win the favor of a kid named Mike, and I smoked weed for the first time at 14 so my brother and his friends we were driving around with wouldn't tease me if I refused. The major difference with these two drugs versus cigarettes was their power to awaken euphoria—that drug high that is so powerful in its ability to erase those negative feelings for a while. Drunk to me wasn't stupor, it was exhilarating and liberating. I felt light and free and, for the first time in my life, I wasn't afraid of everyone around me. The idea of asking a girl to dance didn't inspire terror when I was drunk; in fact, it didn't scare me at all. Smoking weed was different from being drunk, but it did the same thing—it made me not feel, and that's what I wanted.

Author's note: None of this is an attempt to blame my addiction solely on outside forces, nor is it an effort to deflect responsibility for my choices, but I have a huge problem with the idea that addicts choose their path in the beginning or choose to remain addicted because they are weak or lack character. My early decisions to use took place when I was a little boy. I don't know if words can adequately convey the loneliness and emptiness that gripped me. I've heard hundreds of addicts describe this feeling-- they have a huge, empty hole in their chest, and drugs fill that hole up. The notion that I had the ability to understand the consequences of my actions at that age is ridiculous.

The other common misconception about addiction I feel needs to be addressed here is the idea that an addict chooses on a daily basis to remain addicted. I encourage anyone struggling to understand how addicts work to first strive to understand the concept of the involuntary nature of denial and how it enslaves the addicted mind. I did not wake up each day and make a conscious choice to keep killing myself and breaking the hearts of those who loved me. The mind of an addict, in what has been described as an attempt to protect the ego, blinds itself to the day-to-day reality of the addiction. Yes, my use was my choice and mine alone. My addiction, however, once it took hold, lay largely beyond any real choice.

How, then, does anyone ever enter recovery? To me, recovery becomes possible when circumstances conspire to breach the wall of denial behind which the addict survives. Occasionally, the blindness of denial will lift, and a small, fleeting window of opportunity will open. It doesn't usually stay open long, and, if the opportunity to see oneself clearly isn't quickly acted upon, it slams shut. With the power of perfect hindsight, I now see many windows of opportunity that I failed to capitalize on in my addiction, but that failure does not represent a desire or choice on my part to remain an addict. At the time, I just didn't understand them or see them for what they were.

Drug use became the default setting for me when I socialized—if I was with friends, I was always trying to construct a setting in which drug use was possible. I chose friends who would use with me so my doubts about the rightness of using were less troubling. Even when I did find friends that wanted to use, almost none of them wanted to use the way I did. My desire for drugs was limitless—at the end of a binge, when everyone else just wanted to stop for the day and crawl home, I just couldn't seem to turn it off. The only thing that ever stopped my use was money. Eventually, my cash would run out and my credit would dry up, and I'd temporarily have to stop simply because I had run out of options.

As my use increased, cocaine was my main drug of choice. No matter how much money I earned, it was never enough. A business I got involved with in the 80's provided a ready source of cash, and I bled it to the fullest. Of course, cocaine purchased by sloughing off inventory is a sure sign of impending business disaster, but just before the inevitable crash, I was promoted into management. Today it might not make a lot of sense, but in the early to mid 80's there was enough cocaine being used by white collar druggies that even my use blended in. Many of the people I worked with were flush with cash, and cocaine was heavily present when we socialized. One prospective employee who interviewed and trained under me told me years later that he was convinced there was no way he was going to be hired by our company unless he started snorting coke—that's how rampant the use was at the time.

As I said earlier, though, my use always seemed more desperate in comparison. After awhile, I found myself much more interested in getting high than I was in anything else. I was doing a terrible job at work. I constantly lied to my sales force about where I was and what I was doing. I either lied so I could dodge work and get high, or lied so I could dodge work and stay in bed for a few days trying to recover from a binge. When I was conscious enough to have feelings, I was wracked with guilt and self-loathing, and like any good addict, when those feelings bubbled to the surface I just nuked them out of existence with further, heavier drug use.

Eventually, my bosses grew tired of my antics. I was called in and confronted—they didn't know exactly what was causing my shoddy performance, but they issued an ultimatum—fix it or you're fired. Incapable of telling the truth by then, I blamed my behavior on excessive stress caused by the job.

My bosses were good people, and they offered me an out—go see the company psychologist and get some help. When I went to my first meeting with her, we hadn't been talking for more than 10 minutes when she put down her pen and said, "OK. That's enough." Confused, I asked her what she meant. She said, "Here's all you need to know. You're a drug addict and an alcoholic, and you're going to die if you don't check into treatment." When I tried to dodge and manipulate, she rephrased her initial comments with, "You're a dead man. You're just not smart enough to fall over yet."

For those of you who haven't spent a lot of time around addicts, she really wasn't as mean and heartless as she sounds—she just knew that the only way she could quickly break through my years of denial was to shock me, and her words actually had their intended effect. For the first time in more than two decades, I had an honest conversation with someone about the real nature of my use. She agreed to help me, and set about finding me a place to go to drug rehab.

I was lucky enough to work for a company that at the time was willing to pay for a 28-day inpatient drug treatment, and I was doubly lucky to be admitted to McLean's Hospital in Belmont, MA, one of the best drug rehabs in the country. They taught me what I needed to know if I wanted to live. They took me to my first 12-step meeting. For the first time since I was eight, I wasn't doing drugs. It was truly amazing not to want to die every morning when I opened my eyes. It was incredible to not have every word that came out of my mouth be a lie. I no longer had to spend each morning wondering if I was going to puke my guts out in a fit of hangover-induced nausea. Yet, for all the initial relief, there was a long, painful recovery effort ahead.

My initial attempt to get clean lasted for 3 years. By then, I had been clean long enough to start to wonder if I was really an addict. I thought that maybe, just maybe, I had been wrong. I tried to use again in a relapse that lasted a little more than 3 years. My hopes that maybe I wasn't really an addict were very well destroyed at the end of that phase of my use. I had and have a complete inability to use in a controlled fashion. At the time of this writing, I have been clean for about 19 years. I hope that I won't have to relearn the truth of my addiction again—I certainly don't relish the idea of another stint in rehab.

I think it's important, before I end this section, to note how amazingly fortunate I am. There is a common refrain you'll hear if you spend time around addiction: each addict will only decide to get help after reaching what is called a 'bottom.' Many people insist that addicts will only get help if they have been destroyed. I'm sure there's some truth to that notion—people don't check into rehab because they have too many friends or because they're having too much fun. People go to rehab because things have simply gotten too ugly and, most importantly, the drugs have just stopped working. The point at which addicts decide they can't take any more can vary considerably. An addict that enters rehab early in the process is sometimes called a high-bottom addict; one that comes in with just one more breath left in his body is a low-bottom addict. Despite all the suffering I describe, I was a very high-bottom addict. When I got into rehab, I still had a job, I still had a house, my health was not completely destroyed, I hadn't killed anyone, I had no criminal record, and none of my drug associates wanted me dead. Granted, many of the material things were soon to be lost, but I was alive and I was free.

Maybe I'm just a wimp who couldn't take the heat that being a really accomplished drug addict exposes one to, but I'd rather credit my entry into treatment to something less negative—I'm just really lucky. I hear, on a daily basis, stories of heartbreak, destruction, despair and death caused by addiction. My mind boggles that anyone can survive, and often thrive, after going through what some addicts have. I am awed by their capacity to carry on, and I am thankful I didn't have to suffer the lesson at that level of intensity.

4.3 Then and Now--Over Two Decades Later: When I think about the differences between what I was like as a person when I was using addictively and what I am like now as a non-user in recovery, I am most likely to think about my relationships. Family relationships are the most powerful and influential, and family includes first the people you come from and then later the people you join with and create.

When I was using, the only relationship I had that mattered was the one I had with whatever drug I had gotten my hands on. I was willing to sacrifice any personal relationships I had in order to get the drug, and those meant families, friends, loved ones--all were considered expendable when it came to using. There are a thousand different reasons why it ended up this way, but suffice it to say for our purposes here that I felt terrible about myself almost constantly. The only time I didn't feel that way was when I was high, and I never wanted to feel that way, so I tried to stay high all the time.

Of course, if you know anything about drug use on this level you know that emotions can't be effectively fixed by using. Tolerance kicks in, money problems become omnipresent, good relationships turn bad and sick relationships become downright destructive. All this leads to feeling worse than ever, and if you're like I was and drug use is your only coping skill, it soon turns into an ever increasing spiral of use followed by feeling bad followed by more use and on and on and on.

The biggest difference between then and now is how I choose to act when I feel emotions. I'm probably never going to be the poster child for high EQ, but I have picked up a few of the basics. I know that I can't change anything but myself. I know that doing the right thing will not necessarily be rewarded by life immediately changing for the better. I know that being loved is more likely to happen to someone who has the capacity to love. I know that when I feel frustrated, angry outbursts and hurtful comments don't result in a reduction of that frustration but always make me feel guilty afterward. I know that feeling good is not the first step in the process, but the result of a continued striving to be good.

Most importantly, though, is the difference in how I treat my relationships today as opposed to when I was using. When I was using, I simply could not put anyone else first, ever. Granted, today I'm not necessarily that much better, but at least it is in my head that I should try. If someone else cooks, I should clean up. If something is important to my wife or daughter, then I should support that even if its value is not immediately apparent to me.

Finally, it also occurs to me that while I may have been born with certain potentials, that which I became was a person created in the crucible of environment. My emotional environment as a child and young man was an awful, hurtful place. I have the power, as a sober and recovering addict, to make sure that it doesn't happen again. My daughter will never suffer the abuse I did, and she will know every day that she is valued and loved--because I will tell her. Who she becomes is certainly not just in my hands, but largely the environment in which she grows up is, and that is the biggest difference between me then and me now. Today, there is nothing more important to me than my wife and daughter, and that, amazingly, is a place I have found I can be happy.

4.4 Miles To Go Begins

Miles To Go started in earnest on Jonathan's 41st birthday. Kelly was growing weary of the lifestyle of the Broadway bus tour—put on the show, pack it up, drive all night, then wake up in yet another parking lot at another faceless venue. Jonathan was worn down by the demands of being a travelling drug educator--the constant air travel and the not-so-subtle dysfunctional dynamics of 22 recovering-addict educators trying to determine a pecking order. Kelly, always the visionary, had a plan. She was convinced we could take Jonathan's sense of humor, combine it with the story of his addiction and her role as caregiver and fixer of addicts, and with her knowledge of business and dramatic presentation create a better way to do drug education. We spent the next year developing a lecture series about addiction and drugs that was fun, scientific, and medically accurate while simultaneously retaining the power and emotion of our life stories.

We wanted our program to go beyond the slogan-based drug education so popular in that era. For too long, kids had been responding to drug education with rolling eyes and arms crossed over their chests—we wanted to educate, entertain, and engage them. Finally, in September of 1996, with the fundamentals of our program firmly in place, we moved back to California and started teaching. Our program became popular faster than we ever imagined, and we've been at it ever since. We are now, officially, "The drug guys."

Not All Kids Do Drugs
Lessons in Drug Prevention: Handbook One
Proactive Parenting techniques

To order any of our products or services, please visit:
www.milestogodrugeducation.com
Kelly Townsend, M.S. & Jonathan Scott

[i] "Alcohol and Cancer, Alcohol Alert From NIAAA". About.com. 2010. August 22, 2010. http://alcoholism.about.com/cs/alerts/l/blnaa21.htm

[ii] Groch, Judith. "One Cannabis Joint Equals Smoking Up to Five Cigarettes". Medpage TODAY. July 31, 2007. August 22, 2010 http://www.medpagetoday.com/PrimaryCare/Smoking/6298.

[iii] "Youth Drinking Rates and Problems: A Comparison of European Countries and the United States". Join Together. 2005. August 23, 2010 http://www.jointogether.org/resources/youth-drinking-rates-and-a-of.html

[iv] "Drink Like the French, Die Like the French". Marin Institute. August 4, 2008. August 22, 2010 http://www.marininstitute.org/site/big-alcohol/15-industry-tactics/111-the-french-paradox-health-and-alcohol-use-in-france.html?start=8
[v] "Number of Alcoholics". eNotAlone. 2010. August 22, 2010 http://www.enotalone.com/article/5540.html

[vi] Guerrini, I. "Alcohol Consumption and Heavy Drinking: A Survey in Three Italian Villages". Alcohol and Alcoholism. February 14, 2006. August 23, 2010 http://alcalc.oxfordjournals.org/cgi/content/full/41/3/336

[vii] . "Children 'risking liver disease'". BBC NEWS. November 22, 2008. August 23, 2010 http://news.bbc.co.uk/2/hi/uk_news/7743265.stm

[viii] "Fact Sheets, Underage Drinking". CDC. July 20, 2010. August 23, 2010 http://www.cdc.gov/alcohol/fact-sheets/underage-drinking.htm

[ix] "Health Insurance and Substance Use Treatment Need". The NSDUH Report. July 11, 2008. August 23, 2010 http://www.oas.samhsa.gov/2k7/insurance/insurance.htm

[x] "Provide Treatment vs. Incarceration". Join Together. 2010. August 23, 2010 http://www.jointogether.org/keyissues/incarceration/treatment-vs-incarceration-readmore.html

[xi] Akens, Kirsten. "Sample Problems". Colorado Springs Independent. August 13, 2009. August 23, 2010 http://www.csindy.com/colorado/sample-problems/Content?oid=1404779

[xii] "Factors of Teen Drug Use". Adolescent Substance Abuse Knowledge Base. 2007. August 23, 2010 http://www.adolescent-substance-abuse.com/

[xiii] "Drug Abuse and Addiction". NIDA. July 28, 2010. August 23, 2010 http://drugabuse.gov/scienceofaddiction/addiction.html

[xiv] Emery, Chris. "Youthful Media Exposure Holds Promise and Peril". Medpage TODAY. March 1, 2010. August 23, 2010 http://www.medpagetoday.com/Pediatrics/Parenting/18735

[xv] Dalton Ph.D., Madeline. "Relation between Parental Restrictions on Movies and Adolescent Use of Tobacco and Alcohol". ACP American College of Physicians. January/February 2002. August 23, 2010 http://www.acponline.org/clinical_information/journals_publications/ecp/janfeb02/dalton.htm

[xvi] Ibid.

[xvii] "The Importance of Family Dinners V". The National Center on Addiction and Substance Abuse at Columbia University (CASA). September 23, 2009. August 23, 2010 http://www.casacolumbia.org/templates/PressReleases.aspx?articleid=567&zoneid=66

[xviii] "Families, Friends, Schools and Neighborhoods Contribute to Adolescent Alcohol Misuse". Science Daily. November 17, 2008. August 23, 2010 http://www.sciencedaily.com/releases/2008/11/081114080917.htm

[xix] Ibid.

[xx] "Parents Pivotal in Keeping Teens Away From Drugs, Reveals New Data". PARENTS. THE ANTI-DRUG. February 9, 2006. August 23, 2010 http://www.theantidrug.com/news/press-release.aspx?id=19

[xxi] Ibid.

[xxii] "Drug Abuse and Addiction". NIDA. July 28, 2010. August 23, 2010 http://drugabuse.gov/scienceofaddiction/addiction.html

[xxiii] Gilman, SE, et al. "Parental smoking and adolescent smoking initiation: and intergenerational perspective on tobacco control". PubMed.gov. February, 2009. August 23, 2010 http://www.ncbi.nlm.nih.gov/pubmed/19171580

[xxiv] Cartwright, Ph.D., Kelly B. "Effective Behavior Management, Part IV". SelfhelpMagazine. July 7, 2000. August 23, 2010 http://www.selfhelpmagazine.com/article/bahavior-management-IV

[xxv] "Key Findings of the 2008 Partnership Attitude Tracking Study on Teen Drug Abuse". The Partnership for a Drug-Free America. May 1, 2009. August 23, 2010 http://www.drugfree.org/Portal/2008_Partnership_Attitude_Tracking_Study

[xxvi] "Prescription Drug Abuse". MedlinePlus. March 22, 2010. August 23, 2010 http://www.nlm.nih.gov/medlineplus/prescriptiondrugabuse.html

[xxvii] "Prescription Painkillers Becoming More Popular than Marijuana, SAMHSA Says". Join Together. October 30, 2006. August 23, 2010 http://www.jointogether.org/news/research/summaries/2006/prescription-painkillers.html

xxviii "Misuse of Prescription Drugs Common Among H.S. Students". Join Together. June 7, 2010. August 23, 2010
http://www.jointogether.org/news/research/summaries/2010/misuse-of-prescription-drugs.html

xxix "2009 Data from In-School Surveys of 8th-, 10th-, and 12th-Grade Students". Monitoring the Future. 2009. August 23, 2010 http://monitoringthefuture.org/